A hund[...]
    as [...]
happe[...]
    mom? And w[...]

Sarah's shock was beginning to gradually make way for survival mode. She began to wonder what she had to do to stay alive. Should she try and talk to this man? Should she just stay silent?

He told her not to struggle or make any noise. If she did, he would kill her. He then blindfolded her, picked her up once again and took her down some stairs. Even though she couldn't see, she soon realized he had placed her into Stephanie's Jeep. She could feel something in the backseat next to her, but she didn't know what it was . . .

THE GIRL IN THE LEAVES

ROBERT SCOTT

WITH
SARAH MAYNARD
AND
LARRY MAYNARD

BERKLEY BOOKS, NEW YORK

THE BERKLEY PUBLISHING GROUP
Published by the Penguin Group
Penguin Group (USA) Inc.
375 Hudson Street, New York, New York 10014, USA

Penguin Group (Canada), 90 Eglinton Avenue East, Suite 700, Toronto, Ontario M4P 2Y3, Canada
(a division of Pearson Penguin Canada Inc.) • Penguin Books Ltd., 80 Strand, London WC2R 0RL,
England • Penguin Ireland, 25 St. Stephen's Green, Dublin 2, Ireland (a division of Penguin
Books Ltd.) • Penguin Group (Australia), 707 Collins Street, Melbourne, Victoria 3008, Australia
(a division of Pearson Australia Group Pty. Ltd.) • Penguin Books India Pvt. Ltd., 11 Community
Centre, Panchsheel Park, New Delhi—110 017, India • Penguin Group (NZ), 67 Apollo Drive,
Rosedale, Auckland 0632, New Zealand (a division of Pearson New Zealand Ltd.) • Penguin Books
(South Africa), Rosebank Office Park, 181 Jan Smuts Avenue, Parktown North 2193, South Africa •
Penguin China, B7 Jiaming Center, 27 East Third Ring Road North, Chaoyang District,
Beijing 100020, China

Penguin Books Ltd., Registered Offices: 80 Strand, London WC2R 0RL, England

The publisher does not have any control over and does not assume any
responsibility for authors or third-party websites or their content.

THE GIRL IN THE LEAVES

A Berkley Book / published by arrangement with Robert Scott

PUBLISHING HISTORY
Berkley premium edition / January 2013

ISBN: 978-0-425-25882-8

BERKLEY®
Berkley Books are published by The Berkley Publishing Group,
a division of Penguin Group (USA) Inc.,
375 Hudson Street, New York, New York 10014.
BERKLEY® is a registered trademark of Penguin Group (USA) Inc.
The "B" design is a trademark of Penguin Group (USA) Inc.

PRINTED IN THE UNITED STATES OF AMERICA

10 9 8 7 6 5 4 3 2 1

Most Berkley Books are available at special quantity discounts for bulk purchases
for sales, promotions, premiums, fund-raising, or educational use. Special books,
or book excerpts, can also be created to fit specific needs.

For details, write: Special Markets, The Berkley Publishing Group,
375 Hudson Street, New York, New York 10014.

ACKNOWLEDGMENTS

I'd like to thank my editor, Shannon Jamieson Vazquez, for all the help on this book, and my literary agent, Sharlene Martin. I'd also like to thank the Knox County Sheriff's Office and Knox County Prosecutor's Office. And special thanks go to Larry, Tracy and Sarah Maynard.

—ROBERT SCOTT

THE GIRL IN THE LEAVES

ONE

"He's a Real Weirdo"

Relations between Dawna Davis (whose name would often be spelled as Donna in future accounts and articles) and her next-door neighbor on Columbus Road in Mount Vernon, Ohio, had not always been strained. Dawna, the mother of three children, initially liked the young man, thirty-year-old Matthew Hoffman, who resided next door in a two-story house with his girlfriend and her eight-year-old son. In fact, Dawna's eldest son often went over to Hoffman's house to play with the girlfriend's son. The two boys would toss a football around, watch TV and just generally hang out together after school.

Dawna's friend, Leanda Cline, agreed that Hoffman was friendly in the beginning and referred to him as a nice guy. Leanda's son, who would also play over at Hoffman's house, told her that Hoffman let the boys jump around on a trampoline, and made popcorn for them too. They would often sit in front of the TV watching a DVD and eating popcorn.

Dawna and Leanda's sons also had sleepovers at Hoffman's house, and on occasion, Hoffman would give Dawna's fourteen-year-old daughter rides home from the movie theater in Mount Vernon. All in all, he seemed just as Leanda had indicated, "a nice guy."

But near the end of summer 2010, Matt Hoffman began to change. He became more irritable and moody. One day, his dogs suddenly disappeared. Dawna later said, "I believe in my heart that he killed those dogs. He started pulling back and acting strange. I don't know what set him off. He was just getting more and more weird."

Around the same time, Hoffman began setting squirrel traps around his yard. Dawna learned from his girlfriend that Hoffman was catching the squirrels, taking them into his house, butchering them and eating them. On occasion, the girlfriend said, he would even barbecue the squirrels. It freaked Dawna out. She said later, "We liked those squirrels and used to feed them. And then he killed them!"

Dawna quit letting her daughter ride home from the movie theater with Hoffman when she learned he was taking the girl on indirect routes home. These roads ran through sparsely populated areas of woods away from the main logical route back to Columbus Road. Dawna's daughter told her, "We didn't take the main roads back home, we took back roads. It made me uncomfortable."

Dawna also quit letting her son play next door. Hoffman was just becoming "too weird" in her estimation. Hoffman's girlfriend was changing as well. She had initially been talkative and outgoing, but as autumn came along in 2010, she became more reserved and quiet. In fact, by that point, whenever she came over to see Dawna, it was almost as if she had to sneak out of Hoffman's house so that he wouldn't know that she was there. It got so bad that Dawna and Leanda later said that they began to fear for her safety. "We knew something was wrong."

It was more than just a gut feeling on their part. In mid-October an incident brought to light just how much Matt Hoffman had changed from the nice guy next-door neighbor into something else.

Hoffman's girlfriend had finally had enough of his increasingly bizarre behavior and she and her son moved out of his house. She came back one day to pick up some items that she'd left behind, and almost immediately she and Hoffman got into an argument. As it became more heated, she started to leave, but he pushed her over a chair and knocked her to the floor. Then he began choking her.

She later related in a police report, "We were in his living room talking and he got upset and pushed me against a wall. He had his forearm up against my neck and was choking me. I got loose, but he grabbed me again and we tumbled over a chair to the floor. I was fighting to try and get him off of me, but he choked me on the ground."

She estimated that they struggled for two minutes, with him choking her on and off as they rolled around on the floor. Finally he let her up, and they spoke briefly before she left his house. She reported the incident to the police, but then for whatever reasons, decided not to press charges.

After Hoffman's girlfriend and son moved out, Dawna no longer let her children go anywhere near Hoffman. In fact, she wouldn't even let them play in their own yard if Hoffman was outside. He was too erratic, in her estimation, to be anywhere around her children. And his habits were becoming more and more strange.

On occasion he would climb up into the branches of a large tree on his property and perch up there for hours. Just what or who he was looking for, Dawna didn't know. He would also spend great amounts of time in a hammock in a tree. He seemed to be obsessed with trees.

By now, Hoffman gave Dawna the creeps.

As if that wasn't enough, Hoffman, who had always been addicted to computers, had his electricity turned off. Suddenly even that outlet for him was gone. With winter coming on, it seemed crazy to be without such power. But crazy is exactly the word Dawna now used to describe Hoffman. She soon started letting everyone know, "He's a real weirdo."

Matt Hoffman didn't care what Dawna Davis or anyone else thought about him. He had always marched to the beat of a different drum. For example, more than ten years earlier, when he was nineteen years old, he had left Ohio and moved to Colorado, where he had gotten himself into a great deal of trouble. Though he rationalized to himself that he had mainly been the victim of bad luck, that bad luck had cost him prison time and made him a very angry young man.

After his prison stint, Hoffman had moved back to Ohio, where his mother lived, as a condition of his parole. He got a job as a tree trimmer, which suited him. He had always liked being in and around trees. Like his neighbors, his employer at Fast Eddy's, a grounds-maintenance and tree-trimming service in Mount Vernon, at first thought Hoffman was a nice guy. Office manager Sandy Burd later said, "There was nothing strange about him in the beginning. He just blended in. But as time went on, he struck me as really strange. He would just stare off into space."

Not only that, but Burd learned that Hoffman had oversold his tree-trimming experience and had not disclosed that he had been in prison. Hoffman's actions became so troubling that at the end of October 2010, he was let go from his job.

Hoffman was bitter as October turned to November 2010. Now, as Hoffman sat in his house, with no job, no electricity, no gas and no girlfriend, he became more and more angry. He was worked up and agitated, and when he was in such a state, he had to blow off steam. That's when his urges were at their strongest. And the urge right now was as it had been back in Colorado. He liked breaking into people's homes. People who led "normal lives."

He didn't consider himself to be normal. He thought

of himself as extraordinary. The rules that pertained to others didn't pertain to him. When he felt these urges, he was a man of action, and he acted upon them come hell or high water. He knew about a place in the town of Howard named Apple Valley. It was a house that sat alone on a street across from some woods. Best of all, its garage door would not close all the way, giving easy access into the interior of the house. He'd wait until all the people in the house had left for the day, and then he'd sneak inside and take whatever he wanted. Hoffman got a charge out of those kinds of things, and was no stranger to breaking and entering.

TWO

Larry and Tina

1993—CENTRAL OHIO

Fifteen-year-old Larry Maynard was riding his bike down the street in his neighborhood of Reynoldsburg, Ohio, when he spotted one of the cutest girls he'd ever seen. She was blond, petite and athletic looking. Wanting to know more about her, Larry kept pedaling his bike past her block, hoping each time to get another glimpse of her. Before long he learned that she was the same age he was, and her name was Tina Herrmann.

Larry already knew Tina's elder brother, and discovered that she was staying the summer with him, though she usually lived in the small town of Pataskala, which was much more of a farming community, about ten miles farther east. When school resumed in the fall, Larry and Tina started hanging out together every chance they got, despite the distance between their homes.

Along with being cute, Tina was outgoing and popular. She had an infectious laugh and upbeat personality. Lots of teenagers, Larry included, liked being in Tina's orbit. Larry recalled, "There was just something about her that made you like her. Not just me, but lots of kids at school. You hear about someone lighting up a room? Tina was one of those people."

After a few months, Larry and Tina began "officially" dating. They did the usual teenage things—going to movies, sitting down to burgers and fries, cruising around with friends. Though they didn't go to the same high school, Larry and Tina were a couple. She liked watching him play on the football and basketball teams.

Both took school seriously, and Larry and Tina adopted a work ethic early on in life. Neither came from wealthy families, and they realized that no one was going to just hand them money as they grew older. Larry began doing jobs with his grandfather, a professional painter of houses and businesses. And Tina started working at a Kmart store. Soon after graduating high school, they got an apartment together on the outskirts of Columbus.

In April 1997, when Larry and Tina were both nineteen, Tina was rushed to the hospital and gave birth to a baby girl, six weeks premature. Larry was stunned when he heard the news at work. He had not expected the baby to be born so premature. Larry made a beeline to the hospital, where he was presented with his baby daughter, only four pounds, nine ounces, whom he and Tina named Sarah. Larry recalled, "She was so tiny. It seemed incredible that she was alive. She looked so fragile. Sarah changed our world. It was as if our responsibilities had just doubled. I was determined to give Sarah the best life possible."

Larry's mother, Esther Maynard, recalled, "When my son called me to tell me I was a grandma, I thought he was joking since it was April Fool's Day." She was surprised as well that the baby was so premature.

Esther continued, "It was true, however, and my daughter and I hurried to the hospital to see her. Sarah was premature, with lots of wires attached to her. Sarah was a fighter, though, and became strong very quickly and continued to show strength every day."

Despite Sarah's small size, she began to flourish more every day. In some ways she seemed to adopt Tina's vibrant vitality early on. Friends and family "oohed" and "aahed" over her, and she developed a happy quality that became the hallmark of her young life.

Sarah gained more and more weight as each month progressed, and slowly but surely the underweight baby turned into a healthy athletic girl, as her mother had been. Running around the house, getting into mischief, but basically a good, happy child. Sarah was a bundle of energy.

Two years later, Sarah was presented with a baby brother, whom Larry and Tina named Kody. And just like his sister, Kody was also born tiny and premature. But once again, just like Sarah, Kody soon developed into a happy, healthy baby. In no time, he too was a burst of energy, crawling all over the house like a little dynamo.

Larry said, "He turned into a real live wire just like his

sister. Sarah doted on her baby brother. There was a real bond between those two. I was real proud of both my kids. They were also very kind, and they always shared with others. I don't even know how much of that was learned. It was just who they were."

Larry's mother, Esther, recalled that Sarah and Kody both loved bicycles. "We started out with little ones and worked our way up to big kids' bikes. I would watch them ride their bikes up and down the sidewalk until they got tired. They were so happy. I always tried to make sure they knew how much I loved them."

Now, with a growing family, there was even more pressure on Larry and Tina to provide a good life for them. Because neither Larry or Tina had a college education, the prospect of good-paying jobs was limited. Larry looked around and discovered that one of the best paying jobs within his grasp was becoming a long-haul truck driver. The work suited him—he'd wanted to drive a large truck since he was five years old, when he'd sat in the cab of a relative's truck and imagined how it would be to be behind the wheel of such a large vehicle.

Larry knew that he could make a good long-haul truck driver, but he also knew the job would be a double-edged sword. Even though the money was good, it would take him away from Tina and the kids for extended periods of time. At the kids' young age, they would be changing all the time, and Larry wouldn't be able to see those changes for weeks at a time.

Larry recalled, "I began trucking all over America. Mainly because I wanted Sarah and Kody to have a nice home. The company was based in Florida, and I would haul roses and other plants to mom-and-pop florist shops all over the eastern states. I'd also drive out to California and other western states. There were times I wouldn't be home for six to eight weeks, because I'd be driving a load to some place and then picking up another load there. That way, I wouldn't be driving empty trailers on a return trip.

"All of this put a lot of stress on me and Tina. She was working too, at a Meijer's [grocery] store by that time, and also having to raise the kids a lot on her own. It got to be like Tina and I were passing by each other right in our own home. I'd be there for just a little while, and then back on the road again. Even when I was home, I was pretty tired. It was like Tina and I were becoming strangers to each other."

Tina and the kids lived with Larry's grandmother in a nice house in the township of Hamilton, south of Columbus. It was a pretty suburban area surrounded by fields and orchards. The locale had a small-town feel to it, much as Reynoldsburg had.

From Ohio to New York or Florida, from Ohio to California and Washington State, Larry's trucking took him on multiweek runs. He began to know the inside of his truck cab better than he did his own home. There were still good times with the family, trips to the Columbus Zoo, rides for the kids at amusement parks and barbecues. But these times were like islands in an ocean.

Cracks started developing in the relationship between Larry and Tina, and as time went on they became wider and wider. Tina wanted a man who was there to help her raise Sarah and Kody. She felt frustrated and lonely. For his part, Larry wanted to provide for Tina and their two kids but had to be on the road in order to do so. The arguments between Larry and Tina became cyclical and seemingly unsolvable, and they were inexorably drifting apart.

Finally the rift was too large to patch any longer. In anger and frustration, Tina moved out of the house with Sarah and Kody. Larry was devastated. He recalled, "There was real anger between us at first. I felt betrayed and so did she. There was some yelling and accusations. It was not a happy time."

One thing neither Larry nor Tina ever did was use Sarah and Kody as bargaining chips against the other. They both knew that no matter what, they were still the children's parents.

As time eased the bitterness, both Larry and Tina realized that it was circumstances more than character flaws that had driven them apart. At heart, they were both good people who wanted the best for Sarah and Kody, and at some level, they still both loved each other.

Larry said later, "I couldn't stay angry at Tina. She was the first love of my life. She was the mother of my children. There wasn't a mean bone in her body. But the truck driving was just too much for the both of us."

THREE

Sarah and Kody

Tina, Sarah and Kody got an apartment in the town of Hilliard, a suburban area like Reynoldsburg and Hamilton, on the west side of Columbus, Ohio. Even though they were no longer under the same roof, Larry said, "I wanted to see as much of my kids as I could. I was really proud of both of them. They did really well in school, and both Sarah and Kody were very athletic.

"You know how kids can be pretty mean at times. Excluding others from their group. Unpopular kids are kind of pushed to the side. But when Kody saw that kind of thing, he would go out of his way to include those kinds of kids. And he wouldn't allow any bullying around him.

"That was the thing about both Kody and Sarah. They had kind hearts. Maybe it was because they were generally upbeat and happy, that they didn't like to see sadness in other kids. I got together with them every chance I got."

Despite seeing his kids once in a while, Larry was also lonely. In 2005 he met a pretty, dark-eyed brunette named Tracy, and before long they started dating. Tracy had a sweet way about her, was charming and always wanted others to feel comfortable. Where Tina was rambunctious and outspoken, Tracy was quiet and calm. The women, however, did have at least one characteristic in common: a caring nature—they were very loyal to friends and family, and good people at heart.

Shortly after they started dating, Larry and Tracy married and began a new life together. A son, AJ, was born in 2006; like Kody, he was a good and caring boy, and he loved his big brother, Kody, and big sister, Sarah.

Life for Tina was changing as well. She met a man named Greg Borders who worked at the Target Distribution Center where she was employed, and they began dating. After a while they moved into an apartment together with Kody and Sarah in Hilliard, and as luck would have it, they soon had new neighbors down the street— Larry, Tracy and their baby boy, AJ.

By now, any acrimony between Tina and Larry was a thing of the past. He said later, "We had matured by then. And we both loved our kids. We didn't want to argue in front of them or about them. Both Tina and I wanted the best for them."

In a lot of ways it was a convenient situation. Larry got to see Sarah and Kody more often than he had in the past few years. In fact, by 2006 it was one of the happiest times of his life. Larry was driving now locally rather than on the long-distance trips that had taken him away for weeks at a stretch. Larry said, "We'd have Sarah and Kody over for three or four days at a time. I was driving locally, so I got to see them a lot.

"I'd toss a football around with Kody, and we'd do things together like any father and son. I was real proud of my kids. They both did well in school and were just happy-go-lucky kids. Sarah and Kody would squabble about things, as a brother and sister will do, but basically they got along. When Kody played junior league football, Sarah actually became a cheerleader for the team."

Tina's mother, Barbara Herrmann, recalled of Tina around this time, "She was a fun-loving hard worker and very caring mother. She loved dolphins and sunflowers, but most of all she enjoyed watching and cheering on her children as they participated in sports. Kody was a good student and loved playing guitar in his spare time. And Sarah was very athletic."

Everything might have gone along in that manner, but then the economy intervened. The boom times in America were over. In 2008 Tracy lost her job. Soon thereafter, Larry was also laid off. Desperate for money, he decided to take a truck-driving job in Kentucky. Once again he knew it would take him away from Sarah and Kody for long periods of time, but now he had Tracy and AJ to take care of too.

Larry and his family moved down to Kentucky, and he began hauling fuel for a mining company there. His visits with Sarah and Kody were now confined to birthdays and around the holidays. It was disappointing, but times were very lean, and Larry and Tracy were happy to just have a roof over their heads and a paycheck coming in.

This situation went on for about a year and a half, and then Larry was offered a truck-driving job in Florida. Despite being even farther from Ohio, Larry decided that it was worth the better pay and the better environment for his family, so he, Tracy and AJ moved down there.

One day out of the blue, Larry received a surprise phone call from Tina. She said she was thinking of moving down there with Sarah and Kody to live near him in Florida. She said nothing of Greg being part of the move, and Larry assumed that meant she was breaking up with him. Larry was all for this move, since he would be able to see his kids more often. He encouraged Tina to start making plans to move there.

But Tina got other advice from her father. He said she should hang on to the new job she had found after getting laid off in 2008. Good jobs were not easy to find in Florida in a bad economy. Perhaps swayed by this reasoning, Tina decided to stay in Ohio.

She did make one profound move, however. Looking around for a nice area in which to raise her kids, she decided on Apple Valley, an upscale community five miles east of the county seat of Mount Vernon in Knox County, and about fifty miles northeast of Columbus.

Greg, Tina, Sarah and Kody moved to Apple Valley, a picturesque spot located on a beautiful lake. There were several beaches for swimming, and large stretches of water for boating and fishing. Some of the more luxurious homes were lakefront properties, with boat docks and piers. The surrounding area, marked by rolling hills and myriad trees, offered lots of space for kids to run around, and the town had a good school system. It was, simply, a great place for kids to grow up.

Their new home was situated on King Beach Drive, with a large backyard for the kids to play in. It was somewhat isolated from the other homes, with farmland beginning just across the road that ran on one side of the house. Instead of houses across the street, there was a large patch of woods. Nonetheless, the area seemed like a safe environment for the kids. Nothing really bad had ever happened in Apple Valley.

Not only was the location ideal, Tina quickly became very good friends with Stephanie Sprang, forty-one, who lived only two houses away on Magers Drive. Stephanie was just as lively as Tina, and the two got together to go shopping, took turns watching each other's kids, and enjoyed just hanging out with one another. Sarah and Kody would often play with Stephanie's three children. The elder boy, named Michael, was in his late teens; her daughter, Trish, was a little older than Sarah; and her other son, Seth, was younger than Kody. All of the kids got along well, which made the friendship between Tina and Stephanie even better.

Tina and Greg did go in together on buying the house, but there was a downside: while Tina's job at a Dairy Queen restaurant was local, Greg had to drive almost sixty miles each way to the Target Distribution

Center. It meant he had to get up around three in the morning, which was no small inconvenience, but he endured it.

In 2010, Larry's grandmother moved into a nursing home, leaving him the house in Hamilton. He'd always had fond memories of the place, and he and Tracy decided to leave Florida and move there. It was a very nice suburban house with a large yard, and even though Columbus was just up the highway a few miles away, the new home felt as if it was more in the country than in the city.

And as luck would have it, Larry got a job offer to deliver fuel to gas stations in the region. It seemed like an ideal opportunity. Not only would he, Tracy and AJ be able to live in an area they liked, but Larry would again be able to see Sarah and Kody on a more regular basis.

Sarah and Kody continued to do well in school, and Sarah joined the softball team. She was very good at it, and her team even played in a regional competition.

Kody took up baseball and by the age of ten, was an excellent pitcher. One of Larry's favorite photos of Kody was of him winding up on the pitcher's mound.

Tina spent more and more time with her friend Stephanie Sprang. Stephanie, just like Tina, was bubbly and the life of the party. One of Stephanie's cousins echoed Larry's words about Tina when she said, "Stephanie would walk into a room and light it up. She just had that kind of personality. She laughed a lot and seemed like a

happy person. Stephanie and Tina were the best of friends
and did everything together around Apple Valley."

Stephanie had worked at a golf course for many years,
but by 2009 she did odd jobs around Mount Vernon and
Apple Valley to make extra money. One of those jobs
took her to Columbus Road in Mount Vernon to work at
the house of a strange young man. A young man who
liked climbing up into trees.

In August of 2010, Larry and Kody had one of their
most memorable experiences. Kody had always told Larry
he wanted to go night fishing. One evening Larry got
some bait, loaded up an ice chest with hot dogs and soft
drinks and took Kody out to a lake. Larry later said, "He
had a blast. Kody was the only one to catch some fish,
and he was real proud of that fact. And they were good-
sized fish. It was something that was just fun for a father
and son to do. I looked forward to a lot more times like
that with him. Just me and Kody going out to do fishing
or whatever. That August, I thought we had all the time
in the world to do things like that."

There was another trip, in October 2010, that Tracy
Maynard recalled fondly. She said later, "On October 24,
2010, I took Sarah, 13, Kody, 11, AJ, 4, and Payton, 2,
[Larry and Tracy's youngest boy who was born in 2008]
to the Columbus Zoo. It was 'Boo at the Zoo,' a Halloween event for kids. All the kids enjoyed riding the
rides there, and they didn't want to leave until the zoo
closed. On the drive home, we laughed and talked about
everyday things. I dropped [Sarah and Kody] off at their

mom's house and gave them a hug good-bye. I told them we'd soon go to the Wild Lights at the Zoo, which was a pre-Christmas event."

But fate would intervene before that took place.

The small city of Mount Vernon was a picture-postcard kind of town. Compared to the inner city problems of Cincinnati, Cleveland or even nearby Columbus, Mount Vernon's troubles were few and far between. With its large brick courthouse, post office, city hall and churches, it seemed a small-town paradise where residents reveled in a sedate, comfortable way of life. Crime was so infrequent, many people still left their doors unlocked day and night. If there seemed a constant in the area, it was a feeling of contentment.

But there was one individual in its midst who was not content. Matthew John Hoffman was a troubled and angry young man, living in his two-story house on Columbus Road. He felt he'd been dealt some bad cards in his life, and there was a fire burning deep inside him, about ready to burst out of control. And by November 2010, that explosion was only hours away.

FOUR

Young Matt

Even from an early age, Matthew John Hoffman liked being in trees. Like other boys his age, young Hoffman played baseball, but the subject with which he seemed almost obsessed was trees. He loved going out into the woods and climbing them. Perhaps he saw climbing a tree as an opportunity to get away from whatever was troubling him; perhaps he viewed the trees as a safe haven where he could forget the cares of the world, at least for a short time.

Matt Hoffman was the son of Robert and Patricia Hoffman, and grew up in the Warren area of northeastern Ohio. According to his mom, Patricia, he was a good boy, but high-strung. He was smart and had lots of energy, but he was also headstrong and rebellious. When he wanted his way, he tended to dig in his heels and not be swayed in the matter.

Bright and intelligent, he could also be alarming at times. The things he said to people were off-kilter and confusing. If someone said "Good morning" to him, Hoffman was apt to respond with "What's so good about it?" More than one person would later recall how they would ask him a normal question and get "an off the wall" answer in return.

In 1997 Hoffman's parents divorced, and Hoffman moved with his mother to the Mount Vernon area in Knox County. One neighbor, Alice Morelli, recalled Hoffman as a teenager, fourteen to sixteen years of age. She thought that he always seemed unhappy and acted strangely. Morelli said later, "He was really lost. He was on a bad path."

Hoffman did get into trouble around that time, when he and some buddies climbed onto the roof of Lakeview High School. When caught by the police, his only explanation was that he just wanted to see if he could do it. Hoffman would also jump off his own roof onto a trampoline. There seemed to be something about heights that intrigued Hoffman.

Morelli's dog hated the teen, constantly barking at him when he was in the yard. In response, Hoffman would merely stare, blank-eyed, at the dog. It really concerned Morrelli, who thought there was something wrong with the boy. His antics, she felt, went way beyond the usual childhood pranks.

Perhaps unsurprisingly, Hoffman did not take well to

high school, though he did graduate in 1999, and went on to study industrial electrical engineering at Knox County Career Center. Afterward, he went through a long list of jobs in a very short period of time, never seeming to settle down to anything.

In 2000 Hoffman left Mount Vernon and moved to Steamboat Springs, Colorado, where his grandmother lived. The town was about as different from Apple Valley, Ohio, as could be imagined. At an elevation of around five thousand feet, Steamboat Springs was an up-and-coming resort city, geared to outdoor activities, especially skiing. In fact, Steamboat Springs was one of the fastest-growing cities in Colorado. Not unlike Vail and Aspen, it had become a hot spot for both winter and summer sports.

Steamboat, as it was called by locals, had good restaurants, a thriving art scene and lots of new condominiums in town and on the surrounding mountains. Some of the most luxurious new homes in the area were starting to sell for five or six million dollars or even more. These homes were up on the ridge with commanding views of the whole area. People who owned these properties could fly their private jets into the local airport.

Not that Hoffman was living in one of those expensive houses. He was working as a plumber's helper by this time, and his abode in Steamboat was the inexpensive D Bar K Motel. It was the kind of place where a lot of other low-income workers also lived, mainly construction workers, maids and other service-related individuals.

Hoffman was away from his motel room for several

nights in September 2000, however, and his fellow residents at the D Bar K would have been surprised to know where he was spending his time. But it was not long before they found out—along with why he suddenly left the area without any warning. It happened right around the time an expensive condominium caught on fire, and the residents had to run for their lives from the burning set of buildings. Before the ashes settled, Matt Hoffman was long gone.

FIVE

Fire on the Mountain

Around the time of the condo fire, the Steamboat Springs Police Department (SSPD) was aware that three city signs had been stolen from the city park in mid-September 2000, and they were able to trace their whereabouts to unit 6 of the D Bar K Motel. These were not small signs, but rather the large metal and wooden signs that welcomed visitors to the town. It must have taken a lot of effort to remove them, and it had to be done when no one was watching. The local police learned that Matt Hoffman had been the sole renter of unit 6, and upon entering the unit, the officers found one of the signs; the other two were found under the building.

Officer DelValle reviewed the Central Park Management Rental application that Matt had been required to fill out to rent the D Bar K unit. Hoffman had listed his grandmother's phone number on the rental agreement form. DelValle phoned the number and spoke with Hoffman's grandmother. She told DelValle that Hoffman had been in the Steamboat Springs area recently, but had since left. A short time later, Hoffman's mother in Ohio, Patricia, phoned DelValle and asked why the police department was inquiring about her son. DelValle explained the circumstances, and Patricia said she would have Hoffman contact him as soon as possible.

Six days later, DelValle received a voice mail from Matt Hoffman, requesting a call back and giving a phone number where he could be reached in Ohio. DelValle called Hoffman at 5:50 PM on September 14, 2000, and asked if he had stolen three signs from the city park. Unexpectedly, Hoffman said that he had, and that he was solely responsible for their theft. In fact, he gave details of loading the signs into a pickup truck that had a rack and then transporting them to the D Bar K Motel.

DelValle asked Hoffman why he had stolen the signs. His answer was simple: "I wanted some souvenirs from Steamboat." Ironically, however, he hadn't taken them with him when he left town.

DelValle told Hoffman, "Well, you have the opportunity to return to Steamboat on your own accord and expense, or be arrested and formerly extradited." Hoffman said he would return on his own. To this DelValle replied, "You have until September twenty-sixth to do so. If you don't show up, a warrant for your arrest will go into effect on September twenty-seventh."

In passing, Officer DelValle mentioned Hoffman's

confession to Detective Ross Kelly of the SSPD. Ross's ears perked up at Hoffman's name. He knew that Hoffman had been employed by Scott Barnes Plumbing, which had a maintenance contract with Johnson Shipley Management, the company that had provided plumbers for the Ridge Condominiums complex that had burned. Ross also knew that two weeks prior to the fire, which had been deemed a case of arson, a plumber had done some work in condo number 7, the very unit that the arson investigator had since determined was the point of origin for the fire.

On September 26, 2000, Matt Hoffman showed up at SSPD headquarters in Steamboat Springs and Officer DelValle advised him of his Miranda rights. Hoffman signed a waiver of his rights, and DelValle started asking him questions about the theft of the "Welcome to Steamboat Springs" signs.

Hoffman stated that he'd asked a friend at the D Bar K Motel who went by the name "Freedom" if he could borrow his red Nissan pickup truck, and according to Hoffman, Freedom had willingly agreed. So around midnight one night, Hoffman decided to steal the three signs.

DelValle showed Hoffman photos of the recovered signs in the condition they were found. Hoffman looked at the photos and agreed that was the way he'd left them. Hoffman then added that he was glad they'd recovered all the parts of the signs that had broken off when he was removing them from their mountings. DelValle asked Hoffman once again why he'd stolen the signs, and Hoffman replied, "I wanted them for a novelty."

DelValle asked Hoffman what his occupation was, and Hoffman said that until recently he'd worked for the Scott Barnes Plumbing Company. DelValle asked if he'd installed a garbage disposal at the Ridge Condominium, unit 7. Hoffman responded that he and Scott Barnes had indeed installed a garbage disposal there and had also unclogged a tub in a different unit.

DelValle then asked if Hoffman knew there had been a fire at the condominium, and Hoffman said that he did. To this, DelValle asked, "Why would your fingerprints be found on several boxes found in the condo owner's vehicle?" This was a vehicle that had been stolen from the garage of the burned-out condo number 7 at around the same time.

Hoffman replied, "I may have picked up the boxes and moved furniture that was in the way of the plumbing job."

DelValle responded, "Why would you have to move furniture and boxes to install a garbage disposal?" Hoffman didn't answer the question but rather just sat there in silence.

DelValle next asked, "Why were your fingerprints found on the driver's side door of a white Chevrolet Suburban? That Suburban was stolen and filled with property from condo number 7."

Hoffman responded, "I may have touched the Suburban. I went and looked at it."

None of this added up, so DelValle asked, "Why would you go look at the Suburban?"

Hoffman answered, "I found the keys in a drawer in the kitchen. I took the keys and went into the Suburban."

"Okay, so did you drive the Suburban and park it by the Clock Tower building?" (This was a building near the center of town).

Hoffman replied, "I only drove the vehicle on Ridge Road."

To this, DelValle said, "You must know where I'm going with this questioning."

Hoffman agreed that he did, and responded, "Okay, you obviously got me!"

Officer DelValle excused himself from the room and met with Detective Kelly. He asked Kelly to come into the room with a tape recorder and case reports about the condo fire. After a short period of time, DelValle and Kelly went back into the room where Hoffman was sitting. DelValle introduced Kelly to Hoffman and said that Kelly was the investigating officer on the arson fire.

Both DelValle and Kelly began asking Hoffman about items that had been stolen from the condo and placed in the Suburban. Hoffman admitted that he'd taken a stuffed mountain lion, a wood dresser and a bag of clothing from the condo. When asked about a bear rug, antelope head and wooden bench, Hoffman said that he had not stolen those and they must have burned in the fire. Apparently he had left the mountain lion, wood dresser and bag of clothing in the stolen vehicle.

Asked about office equipment, Hoffman recalled that

he'd stolen a fax machine and placed it on the passenger seat of the Suburban, and he'd also taken a small camera. Hoffman continued, "I took items two times, one of which was on the night of the fire. I was in that condo five times. I stayed in there and watched TV because my own place didn't have cable TV. I cooked myself meals and used the Jacuzzi." Hoffman was able to do all of those things because he knew the condo owner was out of town.

The officers asked why he set the fire. Hoffman replied, "I burned the place to cover up the crime because my fingerprints were all over the place. I couldn't have cleaned all the prints. I had no choice. I had to start the fire."

When asked what kind of accelerant he'd used to start the fire, Hoffman replied, "You already know what I used. It was premium gasoline."

The officers wanted to know what containers he'd carried the gasoline in, and Hoffman responded, "Didn't you find the containers? There's always a lot of evidence left after a fire. I used milk containers." Then he laughed, saying that he was just kidding about that. He'd actually bought two plastic gas cans at a local Walmart store on August 26.

The officers wondered where he'd bought the gasoline, and Hoffman said he'd purchased it at a Total Gas Station. Then he drove back to the condo, with the full gas cans, in a red Monte Carlo. Just whose vehicle this was, he did not say. He decided to drive the Suburban to the

Clock Tower building, where he planned to pick it up the next day with all the stolen goods inside. Of course, Hoffman did not have permission to be using the Suburban.

Hoffman continued, "I parked the Suburban, walked back to the condo and sat inside watching television all day. I regretted what I knew I had to do. I watched TV until the early morning hours of the twenty-eighth. I poured the entire ten gallons of gasoline on the floors of all the rooms in the condo and ignited the fuel. Then I immediately walked away."

The officers asked Hoffman if he knew that there were tenants inside the condominium when he set the fire. Hoffman stated, "I knew there were people staying in the [other] units, but the fire alarm would warn them."

Then Hoffman asked if he needed a lawyer. Both Del-Valle and Kelly said that was Hoffman's decision to make, and DelValle brought up the Miranda warning. Hoffman may have thought he was being clever, responding that he'd been Mirandized about the theft of the signs but not about the fire. He may have thought that anything he said concerning the fire could not be used against him.

DelValle, however, explained that the police did not have to Mirandize a person multiple times. Once again Hoffman was asked if he needed an attorney, and he declared, "I've never needed one before, and I already told you everything."

The interview concluded, and the officers asked Hoffman to write out a confession. He agreed to do so, and then he was arrested and transported to the Routt County

Jail where he was held for the theft of the signs and for burglary and arson. Bond was set at twenty-five thousand dollars.

Officer DelValle asked Detective Assistant Kim Gittleson to contact Walmart to determine if two gas cans had been purchased there on August 26. Gittleson spoke with a store employee, who confirmed the purchase of the two gas cans on that date. Gittleson also obtained a printout of the sales receipt.

DelValle contacted "Freedom," Hoffman's alleged friend at the D Bar K Motel; the man declared that he had never "loaned" Hoffman his red pickup truck.

When the list of charges was drawn up against Matthew Hoffman, it included five counts. Count I concerned the arson of the Ridge Condominium complex, and count II dealt with "unlawfully and knowingly" breaking and entering into the condo and remaining there. Count III concerned first-degree aggravated motor vehicle theft, while count IV was about the theft of property from the condo. The final count related to "reckless endangerment" of the lives of the people living in the condominium when Hoffman set the fire.

In a preliminary hearing, Detective Ross Kelly, the condo owner and a criminalist from the Colorado Bureau of Investigation (CBI) lab laid out details of the case. A judge agreed that there was enough evidence for the matter to go to trial.

Hoffman was assigned lawyer David Kaplan, who soon thereafter presented a motion to modify Hoffman's bond. Kaplan wrote in part, "Mr. Hoffman is indigent and without adequate financial resources. The present bond is excessive, and has resulted in Mr. Hoffman's continued pretrial incarceration solely because of his poverty. Consequently, Mr. Hoffman seeks reduction or modification of his bond to a reasonable amount so he can obtain his release from custody."

Judge Thompson ruled that there would be a modification, and ordered the bond reduced to ten thousand dollars. Hoffman was then cautioned not to leave the state of Colorado without permission and to advise the court of any changes of address.

While incarcerated, Hoffman obviously had time to think about his situation, and he came to a dramatic decision: he would not take his chances with a jury trial. Instead, he pled guilty to the charges, hoping for leniency from the judge.

It was indeed a gamble. Each of the first three counts carried a presumptive sentence of four to twelve years of imprisonment and a fine of $3,000 to $750,000. Sentencing guidelines for count IV called for two to six years of imprisonment, and for count V, six months.

On November 3, 2000, Matthew Hoffman signed an agreement with the court that stated he understood the English language and that he had fully discussed his options with his attorney. He also understood the possible penalties for pleading guilty to the charges and agreed that "the decision to enter a plea of guilty is entirely my own choice. There has been no force, threats or promises made to cause me to enter my pleas."

There was another provision listed way down the page, of which Hoffman was aware. It stated, "I understand that I have the right to file a motion for the reduction of my sentence within 120 days after sentence is imposed."

Actual sentencing didn't occur until January 5, 2001, at a court hearing on the matter. Routt County Deputy District Attorney Charles Feldmann called one witness, Jay Muhme, a fire marshal. Muhme spoke about the extent of the arson fire and the resulting danger to the residents of the condominium. Feldmann then asked for a sentence of ten years minimum for Matt Hoffman.

Townsend, a public defender assigned to represent Hoffman in this stage of the proceedings was next; he asked the judge to impose a sentence of six to eight years. And Hoffman had a statement for the judge. He claimed that he now understood the impact and devastation he had caused to others, especially the condo owner's family. Hoffman wrote in part that he'd lost sight of what was most important in life. He thought that money was, but now he claimed, "The A-number-one thing that money can't buy is God. Along with God brings love and the beauty of nature." And then he chose an odd phrase. "These few things are omnivorous and omnipresent in every aspect of our daily routine."

Hoffman stated that he might not have ever come to his senses if it hadn't been for the present "terrible situation. So instead of wishing I didn't get caught, I'm going to appreciate Fate's decision." Hoffman swore that he would learn from this experience and become a better man and useful member of society, declaring that he would take advantage of every opportunity in prison to better educate himself. He promised that he was going to do everything to turn his life around.

In the end, Judge Thompson sentenced Hoffman to eight years in prison, less the 102 days Hoffman had already served. The judge further ruled that Hoffman would be eligible for a boot camp program, an educational/work program within the prison system. If Hoffman was going to "learn from the experience," he was about to get every chance possible within prison walls.

SIX

"Trying to Cut Corners"

Matt Hoffman did not cause trouble in prison and was in fact a model prisoner in the eyes of the system. He completed a Victim Impact Awareness program and received a "diploma" to that effect. He also received a certificate for Intermediate Microsoft Works education.

Hoffman mostly kept to himself and had few friends in prison, though one of those few friends was a fellow inmate named Joe Aldrich, who later spoke of Hoffman as being very "closemouthed" but not a hardened criminal like some inmates. Aldrich thought that Hoffman had made a youthful mistake and was now trying to better himself. He also thought that Hoffman was an intelligent individual who could improve his lot in life once he was out of prison.

It wasn't long before Hoffman was taking advantage of

his right to appeal the sentence, and his latest public defender, Cynthia Camp, helped him in this regard. She wrote, "Mr. Hoffman has no prior felony convictions. Further, Mr. Hoffman has no pending charges or detainers and no history of escape. During his incarceration, Mr. Hoffman has been employed in the janitorial department as a porter."

Camp went on to write about Hoffman's completion of the Victim Impact Awareness program and his enrollment in the Intermediate Microsoft Works program. She also stated that Hoffman's family resided in Ohio and that he'd been in constant contact with them by letter, phone and visits. Camp said that his family was supportive of him while Hoffman was in prison.

Camp declared that Hoffman had a stable work history and had been employed before his incarceration as an electronics and plumbing assistant, golf cart mechanic and dietary aide. He had knowledge in residential and industrial electrical wiring and in carpentry. Hoffman stated he would find "gainful" employment if released early.

To bolster these contentions, Hoffman wrote a letter to Judge Thompson a couple of years into his prison stay. He started out by saying that he had changed since the time of the crimes. "During the crime, although my morals were weak, I did understand the difference between right and wrong. Due to my adolescent ignorance, I did not grasp the magnitude of my actions."

Hoffman wrote that he'd never even thought to consider the impact his crime of arson would have on others.

He said he never would have gone through with it had he realized how devastating it would be: "My assumption was that the insurance company would just take care of the damage and that would be the end of it." Hoffman added that he now realized his actions had deprived the area's residents of their sense of security. He said that he'd hurt the owners of the condominium complex not only financially but emotionally as well. In fact, Hoffman claimed that this realization of the impact his actions had had on his victims bothered him more than his prison sentence.

Hoffman wrote that he'd been raised to face up to the consequences of his actions. And he claimed that's exactly what he'd done when he voluntarily returned from Ohio to Colorado. He stated that his attitude about his role in society had changed dramatically while in prison. Before the crime, he said, he took things for granted. Now, he declared, he no longer felt as if he was just drifting, but wanted to go to college when he got out of prison. With a college degree, he said, he could "put this horrible disgrace behind me."

He went on, "The reason I am pouring my heart out to you in this letter is because you are the only one with the power to give me probation at this reconsideration hearing that is coming up soon. I need to start picking up the pieces of my life and putting them back together."

Matt Hoffman wasn't alone in writing letters to Judge Thompson. His mother, Patricia, wrote that her son had been a model prisoner while located near Las Animas, Colorado. She added, "He is determined to turn his life around and put this all behind him." She stated that in his letters to her, Hoffman spoke of trying to be around people with positive attitudes.

Patricia added, "I am asking that you release him from prison and allow him to come home to Ohio. Matt is lucky to have family that supports him and can help him settle back into society. It will be a great relief to me when he can begin college and get his life back in order."

Hoffman's father, Robert Hoffman, also wrote Judge Thompson, stating, "On behalf of my son, I ask that the court impose a structured release program for Matthew. A guidance program consisting of rehabilitation and counseling in addition to a work release program. In Matt's short life he has caused so much pain and suffering, not only for his victims, but his family and friends and lastly himself. He needs this opportunity rather than continued incarceration."

Hoffman's sister, Melanie, wrote the judge too, saying that her brother had made a terrible mistake. It was one that he would never be able to forget. She added, "I love my brother, and I'm interested in him becoming a productive member of society, learning the skills necessary to live the life of a functional citizen and not an inmate in our country's justice system."

Melanie added that she believed that her brother, if released, could become a useful member of society and could put to use the computer skills he'd learned while incarcerated. She worried that the longer he spent in prison, the more hardened he would become and might "develop the lifestyle of an inmate."

The Routt County District Attorney's Office, by contrast, was unequivocally against an early release of Mathew Hoffman. Deputy District Attorney Elizabeth Wittemyer drew up a seven-point motion against it. Point one stated that a sentence of eight years was reasonable in light of the crimes he'd committed. Point two noted that while Hoffman was declaring a lack of prior felony convictions, that had already been factored into the original eight-year term.

Point three stated that although Hoffman had been enrolled in the Victim Impact Awareness program and computer training, these were not sufficient reasons to lessen his term of incarceration. Point four noted that at no time had Hoffman expressed regret for the danger he'd put tenants and firefighters in when he torched the condominium. Point five brought up the fact that although Hoffman stated he had "come to his senses" and returned to Colorado on his own when presented with the charges, in truth Hoffman had come back to face the charge of theft of the three signs only, not the more serious counts. She declared, "This is a person who was caught and confessed only after he was backed into a corner."

Point six cited Hoffman's claim, made in his interview with detectives, that he'd stolen items from the condominium because he wanted to cut corners. Wittemyer wrote, "Once again, through this motion, the defendant is trying to cut corners."

Point seven addressed the fact that without provocation, Hoffman had robbed and torched a place to cover his tracks. "He put human lives at risk, caused an immense amount of monetary and emotional damage and put a whole community in fear. The People request that the defendant not be allowed to cut any more corners and that he serve his full sentence."

In the end, Matt Hoffman served six years of an eight-year sentence. Typically, a person must serve parole in the county where they committed the crime, which in Hoffman's case was Routt County, Colorado. But Hoffman went back to Knox County, Ohio, to serve his parole.

Once back in Ohio, in 2007, Hoffman had a hard time readjusting, although the difficulty seemed to have less to do with his time in prison than with his oddball personality. He managed to make a few friends and land a few jobs, but sooner or later, people would comment on just how "weird" he was. He made them nervous and edgy.

For a while, though, things seemed to be getting back on track. He got the tree-trimming job and had a good relationship with a new, pretty and personable girlfriend. Hoffman was even able to buy a house on Columbus Road in Mount Vernon in 2009. It cost only $37,500 because it needed a lot of work. Hoffman and his girlfriend and her son moved in, and for a few months everything was fine. But as Hoffman's neighbors later said, he soon began to show very odd traits and to treat his girlfriend badly, culminating in her leaving him in late October 2010. Not long after, he lost his tree-trimming job as well.

So there he was, an ex-con with no girlfriend, no job and bleak prospects. He was by now burning with anger and ready to lash out at the world. It almost didn't matter to him who would bear the brunt of his anger. Somebody was going to pay, and it was going to be soon.

SEVEN

The Intruder

Starting on the night of November 9, 2010, and continuing for the next several days, there would be a marathon of ducking, hiding and weaving on Matthew Hoffman's part. He began it all by parking his car at the Gap Trail parking lot, a few miles from Apple Valley, around midnight. From there he walked to a patch of woods across the street from Tina Herrmann's house on King Beach Drive, arriving sometime around 1:00 AM on November 10. Hoffman already knew that house had problems with its garage door, which would not shut all the way down to the driveway.

Hoffman had some food, a water bottle and a sleeping bag with him. He crawled into his sleeping bag and soon fell asleep. He woke up in time to hear a vehicle pulling out of the driveway of the house very early in the morning, sometime after 3:00 AM. Greg Borders was leaving for work.

Hoffman settled back down in the sleeping bag and fell asleep again. He decided to wait until all the vehicles, and all the inhabitants, had left, and then he would enter the isolated house. It was something he enjoyed doing, and he looked forward to the coming day's activities. Matt got a charge out of being in places that someone else owned, such as the condo in Steamboat Springs.

He also may have known that a pretty, blond thirteen-year-old girl lived in the house. Hoffman would later claim he didn't know that fact, but by that point much of what he said could not be trusted. Whether he knew of Sarah Maynard or not, he was now determined to enter that house whenever he felt it was safe to do so.

November 10, 2010, was just another cool autumn day at Tina Herrmann's home on King Beach Drive. The only unusual thing about it was the activity Tina had scheduled: apartment hunting. Although she was still living in the house with her children, she and Greg Borders were calling it quits as a couple. Tina was now in the process of looking for a new place to reside, and her friend Stephanie Sprang was helping her in the search. They had plans to go together to look at a rental apartment later that day. There was also some talk of looking at a rental house in the area.

The day had begun very early in the household, when Greg left at 3:40 AM for his job at the Target Distribution

Center. Later that morning he spoke to Tina by cell phone while at work, and received a text that the family dog had been fed.

Meanwhile, Sarah and Kody ate breakfast, gathered their school supplies and caught the school bus to East Knox Middle School. Sarah noticed that Kody seemed distracted by something, but he did not tell her what it was. Sarah soon forgot about it and focused instead on the coming day at school.

After the kids left, Tina went grocery shopping at the Kroger supermarket in Mount Vernon, sometime after 9:30 AM. She also bought some gas at the pumps there, and may have even gone to a tanning salon for a while before returning home shortly after noon. She pulled into the driveway, parked the pickup truck she was using and entered her home.

As soon as Tina walked in the door, carrying bags of groceries to the kitchen, a man came tearing out of the hallway and grabbed her. Before she even had a chance to scream, he hauled her to the master bedroom. He was strong and he was in a rage. Against his large frame, 120-pound Tina didn't stand a chance.

The only eyewitness to what happened next was Matthew Hoffman, though mute evidence would tell some of the story.

He may have pushed her down on the bed and hit her in the back of the head with a sap he'd brought along. Or he may have already been reaching for the sharp hunting knife he had with him. In fact, he may have even stabbed her once or twice before he realized another person was in the house. Whatever the circumstances, he was suddenly and unexpectedly interrupted by the appearance of Stephanie Sprang, who had walked into the unlocked house only to find Hoffman bent over Tina with a knife in his hand.

Stephanie's relatives believed that under those circumstances, Stephanie would have immediately rushed the man with the knife to save her friend. This was the Stephanie they knew, someone who would fight anyone to help a friend. And events may have unfolded in just that way. Hoffman, however, would eventually tell a very different story, but regardless, blood evidence would later prove that whatever occurred between Hoffman and Stephanie did so in Sarah's bedroom.

After coming upon Hoffman with Tina in the master bedroom, Stephanie either ran to Sarah's bedroom or was dragged there by Hoffman. Hoffman knew he had to take care of this new woman before finishing off the first one, who lay either badly wounded or dead in the master bedroom.

Stephanie, like Tina, was no match for Hoffman, who overpowered her and stabbed her twice in the chest. The stab wounds were so savage and were dealt with such force that Stephanie died almost immediately. Hoffman didn't stop there, however: he continued to stab Stephanie several more times to make sure she was dead. Her blood spattered the walls and pooled on the floor of Sarah's bedroom.

Then he returned to Tina in the other bedroom and unleashed his full fury upon her. Hoffman stabbed her again and again, puncturing her lungs and other vital organs. He then savagely ripped her midsection with a long tearing thrust. He stabbed her many more times than was necessary to kill her.

After making sure both women were dead, Hoffman dragged Tina's body to the bathroom. As far as he was concerned, his work had just begun. He deposited Tina's body in the tub and, with only a hunting knife, began to dismember her body. This was no easy task, but Hoffman had some hunting skills and was strong. He knew that the knife would not cut through bone, so he disarticulated the woman's body at the joints.

It was an incredibly bloody task, and soon the bathtub and much of the bathroom was covered in blood. Hoffman found some plastic trash bags in the house and deposited Tina's body parts into these. They were not large garbage bags, however, and he had to use quite a few of them.

While he was at his grisly task, the dog in the house would not stop barking. Afraid that the barking might alert someone, Hoffman grabbed the dog, took it to the bathroom and killed it. He then dismembered its body as well and put the parts into garbage bags. Then he turned his attention to the other woman and began to "process" her as well, as he would later put it.

Once finished with the bodies, Hoffman had one more task to do around the house. He found some motor oil and poured it over the worst of the bloodstains and bloody drag marks. He planned to set the house on fire just as he had done to the condo in Colorado, and he figured the oil would burn hot enough to eradicate all the bloodstains and blood trails, even if the whole house did not burn down.

Unaware of the horror going on in their home, Sarah and Kody rode the school bus back to their street that afternoon and walked to the front door of their home on King Beach Drive. From the outside, everything looked normal at the house.

Once they entered, however, the two noticed something odd. They always took off their shoes just inside the front door, and as they stopped to do so now, they spotted what looked to be blood right at the door. It wasn't a lot of blood, but there shouldn't have been any there at all.

Sarah recalled later, "We had a love seat by the door, and Kody was going to take off his shoes there. I saw blood near the door, and Mom wasn't in the house. She always greeted us when we came home."

Concerned about this, they both called out, "Mom!"

Instead of hearing their mom's reply, they were stunned to see a large man come rushing out of the hallway. Before they could even scream, he was on them.

EIGHT

The Girl in the Jeep

As the unknown man hurtled toward them, Sarah just barely managed to slip by him and run to her own room as Kody turned to run out the front door. She slammed her bedroom door and scrambled to find her cell phone.

"He was trying to grab both of us, but [it seemed like] he kind of wanted to do one person at a time. I got by him and ran to my bedroom," Sarah later recounted. It had all happened so quickly, her recollections would be just a jumble of images.

Before she could dial 911, the assailant burst into her room and grabbed her. He had a large knife with him, and in the struggle he cut her finger. Sarah was sure he would now raise the knife and stab her to death. Instead, he sliced through the electrical wiring of a fan in the room and bound her hands together with the cord. Then he told her he would kill her if she cried out.

Sarah remembered, "He was really angry. His voice was like a yell almost. He was telling me what to do. It was like when someone yells at you, and it's a command."

The man found some material to gag her with, and threw her across his shoulder. He was strong, and he carried her down into the basement, where he found an old sled. He cut off the rope that was attached to the sled and bound her legs together. He also put a pillowcase over her head, then hauled her back upstairs and deposited her on the kitchen floor. Before he put her down, the pillowcase fell off her head.

Sarah could not see what he was doing, because of the position she was in, but she could hear him rummaging around for something under the kitchen sink. He seemed to find whatever he wanted, and left the room.

Sarah remembered, "In the kitchen I could see groceries on the floor. It was really weird, because Mom didn't do things that way." Tina kept a clean house, and the kitchen was now in a state of disarray.

A hundred thoughts raced through Sarah's mind as she lay on the kitchen floor. What had happened to Kody? What had happened to her mom? And was this man going to kill her?

After a while he came back into the kitchen and rummaged around again. She could hear water running in the bathroom tub, and every once in a while she could hear the toilet being flushed. The noises from the bathroom seemed to go on and on.

Sarah could see the daylight starting to fade outside the house. The man turned on lights in various rooms and continued doing something in the bathroom. He was in there a long time, and occasionally she could hear what sounded like banging noises.

Sarah recalled later, "When he was in the bathroom, he kept coming out, and he was usually out of breath. He kept opening the fridge. And he kept opening a little cabinet near the sink where cleaning supplies were kept. He got something out of it, and I think he went to the living room. But I didn't know what he was doing. Then he went back to the bathroom, and I'd hear him turn the water on and off and flush the toilet. I didn't know what he was doing, but he did it for a long time."

Her dog should have been barking, but it wasn't. What had he done with the dog? Sarah wondered. Had he let it out of the house, or had he killed it?

Sarah's shock was beginning to make way for survival mode. She began to wonder what she had to do to stay alive. Should she try and talk to this man? Should she just stay silent? None of these questions seemed to have an obvious answer. She would have to play it by ear, see what he had to say and go from there. For a thirteen-year-old girl she was suddenly confronted with some very adult decisions to make.

After what seemed like hours, the man came back into the kitchen. He told her not to struggle or make any noise. If she did, he would kill her. He then blindfolded her, picked her up once again and took her down some stairs. Even though she couldn't see, she soon realized he had placed her in Stephanie's Jeep. She was inside the Jeep in the garage, and he had left to do something else. She could feel something in the backseat next to her, but she didn't know what it was. He came back and put blankets over her, covering her up as best he could.

The man left again but returned a short while later. He climbed behind the wheel of the Jeep and backed out of the garage. By now, it was totally dark outside. Sarah could tell, even through her blindfold, which didn't cut out all light.

The man drove for a time and then parked. He told her to stay where she was and that he would be watching her. He then shut the Jeep door; and she heard him walk away.

Taking a chance, Sarah wiggled her arms and neck, and the blindfold came down a bit. With a shock she realized she was now sitting in the Jeep at a baseball field she recognized, one where her brother Kody had played ball. They were at the Pipesville Road baseball fields. Sarah could also see that there were a lot of trash bags next to her in the Jeep.

Suddenly the man came running back and growled at her, "I told you I was watching!" He pulled up her blindfold and tightened it. Then he said, "If you do that again, I'll kill you!"

Sarah didn't take any more chances. When he left this time, she just sat quietly in the Jeep. Once again she thought about what she needed to do to stay alive. She had no idea if he would take her into the woods somewhere or to a house. Whatever he did, she would have to react to the situation when it came up. Thinking too far ahead wouldn't do her any good at all, she decided.

He was gone for what seemed like more than an hour. Sarah was beginning to get cold. And she was hungry. She hadn't eaten since lunchtime.

More questions raced through her mind. What was the man doing now? Where would he take her? Once they got there, would he kill her? And most of all, once again: where were her mom and brother?

As far as Matt Hoffman was concerned, everything had gone to hell as soon as the kids walked into the house and started calling for their mom. In Hoffman's mind, there was nothing to do at that point but grab them. He'd tried grabbing both of them, but the girl had been too fast, and managed to sprint by him.

The boy was not so lucky. He'd taken perhaps two steps toward the door before Hoffman plunged his knife into the back of the boy's head. The boy died almost as soon as he hit the floor.

As with the two women, Hoffman was taking no chances. He stabbed the boy two more times to make sure he was dead and then raced toward the room where the girl had gone.

He found her in there, trying to make a phone call. Hoffman snatched the phone out of her hand and raised his knife to stab her. But then—he pulled back. Even later, Hoffman couldn't express why he did so. He felt a sudden impulse that he didn't want to kill her.

Instead, he cut a length of electrical cord and tied her wrists together, then told her that if she screamed, he would kill her. He gagged her with some material, slung her over his shoulder and took her to the basement. There, he found some rope and bound her feet. Then he carried her back up to the kitchen and laid her on the floor.

It took several hours for Hoffman to dismember the bodies, put them into garbage bags and pour motor oil on the bloody spots around the home. When he was finally done in the house on King Beach Drive, Hoffman loaded the girl into the Jeep, along with several of the trash bags. He knew what the trash bags contained, but the girl didn't. She was still securely tied up and blindfolded.

Hoffman drove the Jeep to an empty parking lot at the Pipesville Road baseball fields near Howard. He told the girl not to peek, but she disobeyed him, and he caught her. Telling her that he had someone who would be watching her, Hoffman then left the ball field parking lot and walked to the Gap Trail parking lot where he'd left his Toyota Yaris. This took longer than expected. His plan had gone off track very early on and just kept getting worse, as far as he was concerned.

Hoffman got into his Yaris and drove back to where the Jeep was. Since he'd parked it far back in the lot, no one had come by, and the girl and the trash bags were still there, undisturbed.

Hoffman picked up the girl and deposited her into his Yaris. Once again he told her to behave herself and she wouldn't get hurt. He started the engine and drove back to his own residence on Columbus Road. He parked the car in a small alley in back and then, after making sure no one was watching, carried the girl into his house.

His luck was holding so far. No one had seen him bring the girl into the house. Once he had her there, he again told her not to make any trouble for him. He told her there would be someone outside the house watching to make sure she didn't do anything foolish.

After what had seemed like a very long time to Sarah Maynard, the man finally came back to the Jeep. He roughly picked her up and carried her into another vehicle. Even though she couldn't see, she knew they were traveling some distance from the ballpark. It was more than just a few minutes to wherever they were going.

Once the man stopped the vehicle, he picked her up once again and carried her into a house, took her into a room and removed her blindfold. Sarah saw that it was a bathroom, but unlike any bathroom she had ever seen. There were dozens of weird drawings on the walls. They were done mostly in black paint upon a white wall, with figures of people and animals all jumbled together. There was a dog, a bird and a smiling man with a yin and yang symbol on his shirt. There was also a truck that appeared to be a vehicle used in tree trimming. But the strangest depiction of all was a large drawing of a middle-aged balding man. Coming directly out of his mouth was the actual bathroom faucet.

All the drawings and writings looked crazy to Sarah. Obviously this man was crazy as well. Just how crazy, she didn't know. She wondered once again what his plans were now that he had her here. Would he keep her for a while? Would he kill her right here? Or would he take her someplace else in his car?

Hoffman was far from through for the evening. He had the blond girl in his house, but now he had to go back and get rid of all those trash bags sitting in the Jeep he'd stolen and left at the ballpark. Making sure the girl was safely tied up in the bathroom, with duct tape and rope, Hoffman got back into his Yaris and took his tree-trimming climbing gear with him. He had a spot in mind where he could deposit the trash bags, and if he was lucky, they might never be found.

Hoffman drove to a Walmart near Mount Vernon and bought some blue tarp and large plastic garbage bags. He also bought a turkey sandwich, and on impulse, a Halloween T-shirt because it was on sale for a dollar. There was hardly anyone in the store at that hour, which was around midnight. Hoffman paid for his purchases with cash and walked out to the parking lot. All of it had gone smoothly, and no one had been suspicious about his activities.

Hoffman drove away and at around 12:30 AM, parked his Toyota Yaris at a canoe access parking lot on a river. He started walking toward the Pipesville ball field parking lot where he'd left the Jeep, quite a distance away.

Once again, all of this was taking longer than planned. He didn't get there until around 2:30 AM.

Hoffman started the Jeep and drove to a nature preserve miles away. Once there, he had a very good hiding spot. He was sure no one would ever find where he was about to put all those trash bags. If his luck held, no one was ever going to know exactly what had happened at that home on King Beach Drive. And in one regard he had been lucky: Greg Borders was gone all day and night. After work on November 10, Greg spent the night at a friend's house, and on November 11, the two went golfing.

For Hoffman, meanwhile, time was moving on. After getting rid of the trash bags, he drove the Jeep back to the house on King Beach Drive and swapped it for the pickup truck that was there. His intention was to get a couple of gas cans, fill them with gasoline and bring them back to the Herrmann house. For some reason, he left the extra trash bags and blue tarp that he'd just bought at Walmart in the garage. This may have been because he intended to come back and burn the whole place down, but that part of his plan did not work out. The pickup truck was having problems and would not stay in gear. It bumped and jerked down the road, and Hoffman didn't want to be pulled over by some policeman.

Finally, in frustration, Hoffman abandoned the pickup truck in a parking lot near a place called the Brown Family Environmental Center, close to Kenyon College, in the small town of Gambier. From there he started walking once again and did not reach his Toyota Yaris until around dawn.

Instead of going back to burn down the house on King Beach Drive, Hoffman returned home. He was exhausted by now. Hoffman went inside his house and looked in the bathroom. The girl was still tied up and lying on the bathroom floor. It was time to deal with her.

NINE

A House of Leaves

When Tina Herrmann did not show up for her job at Dairy Queen in Mount Vernon on the afternoon of November 10, 2010, her friend and manager at the restaurant, Valerie Haythorn, called the Knox County Sheriff's Office (KCSO). Not showing up to work was unheard of for Tina; she was very responsible, and had never done anything like this before. Valerie was sure that something bad had happened to her.

Valerie talked to a dispatch operator at KCSO in the early evening hours and explained her concern. The operator told Valerie that a sheriff's deputy would go by Tina's house to do a welfare check, to determine if anything seemed out of place, or whether a dangerous situation might have occurred.

Knox County Sheriff's Deputy Charles Statler was

contacted about Valerie's call and told to do a welfare check on Tina Herrmann on the 400 block of King Beach Drive. Statler in his report noted, "Valerie advised that Tina did not show up for work today, and she is concerned that something may have happened to her because Tina was going to break up with her boyfriend Gregory Borders."

Deputy Statler drove by the house shortly after 8:00 PM and noticed that there was no vehicle in the driveway and no lights on in the house. He rang the doorbell, but no one answered. Since he didn't have a search warrant to enter the house, and nothing outside seemed amiss, he noted the situation—the lack of a vehicle in the driveway and the lights off in the house—but didn't see further cause for investigation.

Though he didn't have to, Deputy Statler made a second welfare check at around 11:15 PM. This time, he noted the interior lights of the house were on and that a blue 2004 Ford pickup was parked in the driveway. Once again, however, nothing seemed to be amiss at the residence.

Deputy Statler didn't know it at the time, but the man who lived with Tina, Sarah and Kody, Greg Borders, was out of town for the night. And as far as Stephanie Sprang went, apparently, no one in her household was concerned for her safety at that point. They may have thought that she was spending the night with Tina, or perhaps was even out of town with her. No one reported Stephanie as missing.

*   *   *

Back at Matthew Hoffman's house, Sarah tried to stay awake during the night, but the whole ordeal had been too exhausting. She found herself drifting in and out of a nightmarish sleep. Already her sense of time was starting to slip away. After what she guessed must have been many hours, the man who had kidnapped her returned to the bathroom where she lay on the floor.

He made sure that her restraints were still in place, and Sarah began to put into practice what she knew would be a very delicate but important fight for her life. She decided that she had to befriend him. "I have to get him on my side," she thought, realizing that might be the only way to keep him from killing her. By this time, she had suspicions about what exactly he'd done to her mom and Kody. She was unaware, however, that Stephanie Sprang had also been in her mom's house and had been murdered as well.

After some innocuous chitchat, Sarah asked Hoffman about the strange drawings on the wall. His answers didn't make much sense to her, but she tried to follow what he said. He tried to explain to her about the characters drawn on the wall, some of them human, some of them animals, and some half-human, half-animal. She asked if he was an artist. He did not reply.

After a while the man took Sarah out of the bathroom; she was not blindfolded at that point. She looked around and was stunned. There were bags and bags of leaves stacked up in every room, and a layer of leaves was spread out on the floors of the rooms, almost like a carpet.

Sarah asked, "Why are there so many leaves in the house?"

The man replied, "I use them to keep the house warm. They're insulation."

Sarah didn't know if he was lying about this or not, but it seemed like a very odd way of insulating a house.

Changing gears, Sarah asked, "Did you break into our house before?"

The man answered no.

"How did you get to our house?" She wanted to know this, because obviously he had not driven her away from the house in his own car, but rather in Stephanie's Jeep.

The man answered, "I had someone drop me off there."

Sarah did not quite believe him, but she didn't press the issue.

She then asked, "Did you kill my mom and Kody?"

The man said, "No."

She was very skeptical about this as well but didn't question him further about it. Instead she asked, "What did you do to my dog?"

The man said, "I let it out of the house." This, of course, was a lie. The dog was dead, its body parts stuffed into bags along with those of Tina, Stephanie and Kody.

By now Sarah was starving. She asked if he could feed

her something. His answer surprised her. "I have some dead squirrels in the freezer. Do you want me to cook you up one?"

Sarah replied, "No!" She would rather go hungry than eat squirrel.

Finally he made a bowl of cereal for her. But the milk was sour, and it took a lot of control on her part not to gag and spit out the awful stuff. If this was all he was going to give her to eat, she knew she had to make the best of it.

Hoffman would say later that he was exhausted, so he tied the girl to him and fell asleep on a couch. Sarah adamantly denied this account, saying that Hoffman once again gagged her and kept her tied up where she could not get away. He also stuffed her in a closet at some point, though later on, both Hoffman's and Sarah's memories were so disjointed, it was hard to know when certain events had happened. Whatever the case, Hoffman took a much-needed nap to recoup after all his excursions during the night. He knew he'd need his strength to perform the many tasks necessary to keep himself in the clear.

When Tina Herrmann failed to show up to work on Thursday, November 11, her friend and manager Valerie Haythorn was so concerned that she again phoned KCSO. Sergeant Al Dexter learned from a phone call to Sarah and Kody's school that they had not shown up either that day. All of this was becoming more worrisome. It was not like the kids to skip school.

A short time later, Valerie phoned KCSO once more and told them that she'd just learned that Tina's friend and neighbor, Stephanie Sprang, was also missing. Valerie had phoned Stephanie's house because she knew that Tina and Stephanie were such good friends. It was at that point that Valerie learned Stephanie was missing as well. Sergeant Dexter did a welfare check at Stephanie's residence and another check outside of Tina's residence. No one was at home at either place when he arrived. Sergeant Dexter also noted that the blue Ford pickup that Deputy Statler had seen in the driveway the night before was now gone from the area.

Around 4:00 PM, Valerie managed to contact Stephanie Sprang's live-in boyfriend, Ron Metcalf, and they agreed to meet and check Tina's residence. Ron lived with Stephanie on Magers Drive, only a few houses down the road from Tina's place. When Valerie got there, she and Ron talked for a while, and then Valerie decided to enter the house. She removed a rear window screen, raised a window and climbed through. Everything was very still, quiet and spooky. Valerie went farther into the house, and what she saw terrified her: there were bloodstains on the living room and hallway carpet, a lot of blood. It looked as if someone had been dragged along the carpet. Valerie, now frantic, quickly left the house and phoned the sheriff's office once more.

Previously, the officers had been sent to do only "welfare checks," but now it was clear there was something seriously wrong at the house on King Beach Drive. This time, when KCSO sergeants arrived at the residence, they were determined to go inside and figure out just what had happened there.

TEN

A Chance Encounter

David Barber had been the sheriff of Knox County, Ohio, for eighteen years by November 2010. He was one of those guys who had come up through the ranks. Before becoming sheriff, he'd been a uniformed deputy sheriff, a detective, a detective sergeant and the lieutenant in charge of the detective division at the KCSO.

He'd won numerous awards over the years, including Ohio's Distinguished Law Enforcement Service Award in 1999. He was very proud of his office having received CALEA accreditation in July 2007. CALEA stood for Commission on Accreditation for Law Enforcement Agencies, which had been created in 1979 as a credentialing authority through the joint efforts of law enforcement's major executive associations. CALEA's goals were to "strengthen crime prevention and control capabilities, formalize essential management procedures, and establish fair and nondiscriminatory personnel practices." It was also to "solidify interagency cooperation and coordination and increase community and staff confidence in the agency." In layman's terms, being accredited by CALEA helped KCSO work more smoothly with other law enforcement agencies in cases of an emergency where a lot of police presence was needed.

Sheriff Barber had no idea on the morning of November 11, 2010, that in a very short amount of time he and his office were going to need all the benefits CALEA accreditation had to offer. All he knew then was that KCSO was the smallest sheriff's office to ever achieve CALEA standards.

Despite the sheriff's rightful pride in the accreditation, he did not regularly need to go outside his own department for help. Crime in Knox County was simply not prevalent. In the preceding year there had been only one confirmed robbery, one stabbing, one kidnapping case, and one homicide. Even the number of vehicle thefts had totaled only thirty for the whole year.

Because of Valerie Haythorn's initial phone call to KCSO, the first officer to have had any contact with the King Beach Drive residence was Deputy Charles Statler of KCSO's Patrol Division.

The Patrol Division, headed by Captain David Shaffer and comprised of three sergeants and eighteen deputies, was responsible for protecting the sixty thousand people in the county, spread out over 525 square miles. Cities like Mount Vernon had their own police departments, but all the rural areas, including Apple Valley, where Tina, Sarah, Kody and Stephanie lived, were patrolled by KCSO units.

Because of the disturbing circumstances at the home on King Beach Drive, the matter was taken on by the KCSO Detective Division. This division was headed by Lieutenant Gary Rohler, and included Detective Sergeant Roger Brown, and Detectives Thomas Bumpus, David Light and Doug Turpen. Prior to that November, almost all the deaths investigated by the KCOS detectives were the result of accidents.

On November 11, 2010, the detectives weren't quite sure what they had on their hands at King Beach Drive. It became case number 10-2071, and one of the lead investigators was Detective David Light. He noted early on, "Deputy Chuck Statler tried to contact the residence but was unable to contact anyone. On Thursday, November 11, 2010, officers were again unable to make contact and also found that Tina [Herrmann]'s children, Sarah and Kody Maynard, did not go to school November 11th."

After Valerie Haythorn's discovery of the blood in the house on King Beach Drive, Sergeants Tom Durbin and Al Dexter of KCSO were sent to Tina's house to investigate. The sergeants entered the house looking for someone who might be injured, but what they found was extensive amounts of blood on the front room carpet and what appeared to be bloody drag marks to the bathroom.

There was also blood in the basement and a Jeep that did not belong to Tina in the garage.

The sergeants immediately called for KCSO detectives. Detective Light responded, as did Detective Sergeant Roger Brown. Brown noted that he arrived at Tina's house at 4:36 PM on November 11, and met with Sergeants Durbin and Dexter in the yard. The area around Tina's house was soon secured with crime scene tape.

Detective Light called Stephanie's house, and by that time someone was home. Light noted that Tina's friend, Stephanie Sprang, was also missing. Stephanie's live-in boyfriend, Ron Metcalf, told detectives that neither he nor Stephanie's children had seen or heard from her since 12:30 PM on Wednesday, November 10, when Ron had last spoken to her by phone. Ron told Detective Sergeant Brown that Stephanie had not been home when he arrived there later on November 10. Ron added that he'd made several attempts to reach Stephanie via her cell phone, but had only gotten her voice mail.

Ron also informed Detective Sergeant Brown that Tina and Stephanie had had plans to look at apartments the day before, because "Tina was going to leave Greg and move out." Tina and Stephanie were supposedly going to look at an apartment complex owned by a man named Tony, though when Brown contacted Tony, he claimed he had never heard from either woman about renting an apartment.

After the discoveries at the house, Detective Sergeant Brown contacted Knox County Prosecutor John Thatcher and requested that he prepare a search warrant. Thatcher replied that if Brown could find Tina's boyfriend, Greg Borders, he could get permission to search from him.

As it turned out, Brown didn't have to go looking for Greg Borders. Greg arrived at the house on King Beach Drive at 5:30 PM. Greg explained to the detectives that a family member had told him about the police activity at his house and he'd hurried home to find out what was going on. Apparently Greg hadn't had his cell phone on earlier, and had been unaware of the police presence until he'd gotten word about it from an uncle.

Greg explained to the officers that he'd left the residence on November 10 at 3:00 AM to go to work. Greg said that he worked throughout the day and then stayed with a friend that night. Greg added that he and his friend had been golfing all day on November 11, and he hadn't seen Tina since he went to bed on November 9.

Detective Sergeant Brown read a KCSO Permission to Search form, and Greg said that he understood it and signed the document. Brown then instructed Greg to remain on the back porch, and he and Lieutenant Gary Rohler entered the house by an unlocked back door. Whether Valerie Haythorn had unlocked that door on her way out, or an assailant had, the detectives didn't know at that point. Brown later documented what he saw: "As I looked into the kitchen and living room areas, I observed what appeared to be blood and drag marks on the living room carpet and what appeared to be blood on the linoleum at the top of the basement stairs. At this time, Lt. Rohler and I exited the residence to await

BCI&I Crime Scene Agents." BCI&I was Ohio's Bureau of Criminal Identification and Investigation.

Brown next received verbal consent from Greg Borders to examine his arms, hands and torso for scratches and injuries. After the examination, Brown noted that Greg did not appear to have any injuries on him.

The actual affiant for the search warrant, the person responsible for detailing the warrant's purpose, was KCSO Detective David Light. Even though Greg Borders had given a verbal okay to search the residence, it was best to have a written search warrant signed by a judge. Detective Light began by stating that he had been with KCSO since 1993 and had been a detective since 2008. In his time with the sheriff's office, he'd investigated twelve cases involving felonious assault, one kidnapping and twenty deaths.

The main part of Light's search-warrant request included the lines, "At approximately 4:15 PM on November 11, 2010, Sergeant Tom Durbin and Sergeant Dexter responded to Ms. Haythorn's call, entered Ms. Herrmann's residence where they observed bloodstains on the living room and hallway carpet, apparent drag marks in the bloodstains on the hallway carpet going in the direction of the bathroom and a large amount of blood around the tub and toilet area. And they observed a gallon jug of what appeared to be [motor] oil in the hallway with a ten inch trail of liquid leading from the hallway to a bedroom." In fact, the motor oil had been dripped on the rugs in several portions of the house.

Light added that Sergeants Durbin and Dexter had also observed bloodstains going down the stairs to a lower-level garage where a light gray or green 1996 Jeep Cherokee with Ohio plates was parked.

The Jeep Cherokee was known to be driven by Stephanie Sprang, but the registration listed a man named Jeremy Biggs as the owner. Just how Biggs fit into all this, the investigators did not yet know.

KCSO deputies spread throughout the neighborhood, questioning neighbors about the missing individuals. Investigators noted immediately that no houses were right next door to the King Beach Drive address—it was fairly isolated, with a patch of woods across the street and farmland across Magers Drive.

Even before the search team began processing Tina Herrmann's house, miles away Matt Hoffman was deciding to put into action his plan to burn down the house on King Beach Drive.

After first making sure that Sarah Maynard was completely restrained and could not get away, sometime after 6:00 PM on Thursday, November 11, Hoffman drove his Toyota Yaris back to Gambier near Kenyon College and the parking lot where he had left Tina's blue pickup truck. He was going to collect the gas cans from the truck, fill them up with gasoline and then go to the residence. But before he could access the pickup, fate intervened.

Hoffman had abandoned the pickup at the Kokosing

Gap Trail parking lot off of Laymon Road and State Route 229, an area used as a launching spot for canoes on the Kokosing River. At 6:55 PM, KCSO Deputy Aaron Phillips was driving around on his routine patrol when he spotted the blue pickup truck. Deputy Phillips already knew that Deputy Charles Statler had spotted a similar pickup truck in Tina Herrmann's driveway at around 11:15 PM on November 10. What was it doing here now?

Then Deputy Phillips spotted something else unusual. There was a silver car parked near the edge of another nearby lot, even though the lot was now closed for the night, and a man was sitting in the car behind the steering wheel.

Deputy Phillips approached the vehicle and asked the man what he was doing there and asked to see his driver's license. The man cooperated and handed over his license. Deputy Phillips checked it and noted that the driver was Matthew Hoffman who lived on the 3000 block of Apple Valley Drive, and that his driver's license had just been renewed on October 26. Phillips asked Hoffman if the Apple Valley Drive address was close to King Beach Drive, and Hoffman said that his mother lived there, but added that he now lived at 49 Columbus Road in Mount Vernon. Asked once again what he was doing there, Hoffman said that he was waiting for his girlfriend, Sarah.

The name Sarah didn't mean anything to Deputy Phillips at that point, and he told the young man the parking lot was closed after dark. Hoffman said okay and left.

* * *

The incident with Deputy Phillips had effectively thwarted
Hoffman's plan to retrieve the gas cans from the pickup
truck. Hoffman felt as if he'd dodged a bullet at the parking lot, though, at least law enforcement officers weren't
looking for him—yet. But time was ticking away and he
still had to burn down the house and all the incriminating
evidence inside.

Since Hoffman didn't want to drive his Yaris directly to the house on King Beach Drive, he returned
home to think over what his next move would be. Not
only was there a problem with his entering that house,
but he'd also left several items in the woods across the
street from the house. What if officers decided to look in
the woods? He had to retrieve those things, or they
could lead directly back to him. Matthew Hoffman had
a lot more work to do before all of this was over.

ELEVEN

A Footprint in Blood and Oil

Because Tina's pickup truck had been found so close to Kenyon College in the town of Gambier, the school was put into a state of lockdown. At 10:15 PM November 11, e-mails and phone calls were sent out to students and faculty. All of the messages warned people to stay in place, which meant no wandering around the campus grounds. Students not already in their dormitories were escorted there by campus security officers. Students residing at the Brown Family Environmental Center, near where Tina's pickup had been found, were transported to Weaver Cottage on the Kenyon campus.

Additional campus security officers were brought in to help secure the campus, and the sixteen hundred students cooperated during the lockdown. Mark Ellis, communications director for Kenyon College, later said, "We were contacted by the Knox County Sheriff's Office, who [informed us] of a crime at Apple Valley and the possibility that a dangerous person might be on campus." This lockdown was taken seriously by students and faculty.

Back at the Kokosing Gap Trail parking lot, investigators were busy taking multiple photos of Tina Herrmann's pickup truck and scouring the surrounding area for evidence. Once they finished the onsite investigation, they loaded the pickup onto a car carrier and took it to a police impound yard. There it would be searched in a more thorough manner under very controlled conditions. Of vital interest to the investigators was whether any blood could be found in the pickup, as well as any fingerprints that did not match those of Tina, Sarah, Kody or Stephanie. Meanwhile, Hoffman moved Sarah down into his dark basement and onto a bed of leaves that he had constructed for her, and removed her blindfold. She recalled later, "I was really afraid when I was first taken there. It was so dark, you couldn't see anything. There were no windows, so you couldn't tell if it was day or night.

"He would come down there sometimes and just stand there and stare at me. He didn't say a word, just stared. And then he would go back upstairs. I don't know which was worse—him not saying anything or him saying something. I couldn't figure out what he wanted when he didn't say anything. It was hard to tell what he was thinking that way. Mostly I just laid alone in the dark.

And even though there were blankets and stuff that he put there, it was always cold. At least it was better than lying on the floor [of the bathroom] where he first kept me. That was not only cold, it was hard too.

Even though it was almost impossible to keep her thoughts from conjuring up frightening images of what might happen next, she later said that she tried to suppress these thoughts as best she could. Her plan was to only deal with whatever was happening at the moment. Especially when it came to interacting with her captor.

While Hoffman was planning his next move, BCI&I Special Agents Edward Lulla and Edward Carlini arrived at Tina Herrmann's residence on King Beach Drive. It was 9:45 PM on Thursday, November 11. Outside the house, they were briefed by KCSO Sheriff David Barber and several KCSO detectives, who gave the BCI&I agents all the background on the incidents that had led up to the request that they be there: the report by Valerie Haythorn, the blood in the house and the missing individuals.

Sheriff Barber added that a KCSO patrol deputy had spotted the pickup truck that Tina usually drove, in a parking lot of the Kokosing Gap Trail. The pickup truck had been towed to a storage yard for analysis.

After the briefing, Agents Lulla and Carlini and Detective Sergeant Roger Brown pulled on protective footwear over their shoes and entered the residence. During their initial run-through, they noticed that the garage door was off its track. They did not know whether this was something new or had been that way for a while.

Given that it looked to be a very complex crime scene, Agents Lulla and Carlini requested that BCI&I Special Agent Gary Wilgus join them to do any blood-spatter analysis. Wilgus, however, told them he couldn't make it there until the next day, so the two other agents decided to start doing some of the processing before he arrived.

In the initial walk-through, Agents Lulla and Carlini noted "a remarkable amount of blood in three separate areas of the house, each [of] which led to the main bathroom of the house. In the bathroom were large stains and a bathtub and shower wall covered in suspected blood."

Both Agent Lulla and Carlini worked until 4:00 AM, November 12. Because of the very late hour, it was decided that the residence would be secured by KCSO, and the BCI&I agents would return again later in the day.

When he returned to his house following the incident with Deputy Aaron Phillips at the Kokosing Gap Trail parking lot, Matt Hoffman made sure that the girl was tied up on the bed of leaves in the basement and then decided to drink a bottle of wine and burn some incriminating evidence. He started a bonfire in his backyard and threw his shoes into the flames. This didn't seem to concern his neighbors, since they were used to him doing odd things at all hours of the day and night. Hoffman made sure that the shoes burned down to ash. He wasn't worried about the girl in his house—she was tied up and gagged. He then slept for a couple of hours and woke around midnight. Before he left, he went down to the basement and looked at the girl again. He didn't say anything, just stared at her.

In the early hours of Friday, November 12, Hoffman decided to go back to the woods near Tina's house, the same woods where he had spent the night of November 9. He'd left items there he now needed to collect before the police found them. He also wanted to see what kind of police activity was going on at the residence on King Beach Drive.

Hoffman drove to a parking lot at Millwood and then rode his bike to a hill near Apple Valley Lake. From there he left his bike and slowly made his way on foot to the woods near Tina's residence. It was miles away, and once again this took a lot of time.

When he arrived, in the darkness of the early morning hours, Hoffman noticed the crime scene tape around the house and the police working, both inside and out. Hoffman spent awhile in the woods, watching. In some ways he liked this—seeing what they were doing and not being seen. The police seemed to have no idea he was down there spying on them. Hoffman got a kick spying on people—he had often done so from up in the branches of a tree on his property,

After quite a while of watching, Hoffman gathered up a few of his things before making his way back, on foot, to his bike and then backtracking to his car. Authorities would learn later just what he took from the woods—a baseball cap and a knife—and what he left behind. And as with much of what Hoffman did, none of it would make much sense to other people. The walk to his bicycle took quite a long time, and it was about 9:00 AM when he got home, once again exhausted from all his nocturnal activities.

Sarah, left in her cold dark dungeon on the bed of leaves, was fairly certain that her captor was gone once again. But he had told her that someone else would be watching the house whenever he wasn't there. And besides, what could she do? She was tied to the primitive frame of the bed of leaves.

Sarah believed Hoffman was telling the truth about an accomplice. How else could he have moved so many vehicles around by himself? And how had he gotten to her house in the first place, if someone had not dropped him off there? Obviously he had driven Stephanie's Jeep away from the house, with her in it, and she had even seen the silver car he'd approached, parked at the Pipesville Road baseball fields.

Sarah decided not to cause any waves. If someone was indeed watching the place, she didn't want anything bad reported back to her assailant. It was best to do just what he said. It was her best insurance of survival.

TWELVE

A Scene of Horror

Special Agent Gary Wilgus of BCI&I met with Agents Ed Lulla and Ed Carlini at Tina's residence at 1:00 PM on Friday, November 12, 2010. Sheriff David Barber was there also, along with Detective Sergeant Roger Brown and several deputies who were securing the scene. The BCI&I agents and Detective Sergeant Brown put protective coverings over their shoes and entered the house.

Wilgus was briefed by the other agents, and his job would now be to examine the blood-spatter patterns while Agents Lulla and Carlini processed Stephanie Sprang's Jeep Cherokee, which was still parked in the garage.

Agent Wilgus was a bloodstain expert, and early in his report he defined the terms he would be using to describe his findings. A "bloodstain" was a deposit of blood on a surface. An "altered stain" was a bloodstain with characteristics that indicated a physical change had occurred. A "blood drop" was a volume of blood of sufficient weight to overcome its surface tension and fall free from the mass of blood from which it was formed.

Wilgus defined a "drip stain" as a bloodstain resulting from a falling drop that formed due to gravity. And an "impact pattern" was a bloodstain pattern resulting from an object striking liquid blood. A "perimeter stain" was an altered stain that consisted of the peripheral characteristics of the original stain. A "saturation stain" was a bloodstain resulting from the accumulation of liquid blood in an absorbent material.

A "spatter stain" consisted of a bloodstain resulting from a blood drop dispersed through the air due to an external force applied to a source of liquid blood, as might result, for example, from someone being struck by a heavy object. A "swipe pattern" was a bloodstain pattern resulting from the transfer of blood from a blood-bearing surface onto another surface, with characteristics that indicated relative motion between the two surfaces. "Transfer patterns" were contact bloodstains created as a result of compression or lateral movement of a bloody surface against a second surface. And a "wipe pattern" was an altered bloodstain pattern resulting from an object moving through a preexisting wet bloodstain.

The different types of bloodstain patterns had important meaning to someone as trained as Special Agent Wilgus. The patterns could tell him to a great degree what had happened in certain locations, and enabled him to reconstruct a chain of events.

Agent Wilgus went to the vinyl foyer floor inside the front door and began to note different bloodstains there. He carefully looked at "several patterns of interest" on the vinyl floor area at the entrance. The first, and largest, of the stains was a transfer pattern found immediately in front of the door, and there were perimeter stains located at the southeast corner of the vinyl floor. He also picked up a wipe pattern after using Leuco Crystal Violet, or LCV.

The transfer pattern was consistent with a blood-stained object having come into contact with the floor. The pattern was ten inches long and six inches wide. Also scattered on the vinyl floor were blood drops that appeared to be altered or diluted, more transparent than typical blood drops.

Moving on to the carpeted area of the living room, just south of the front door, Wilgus noticed a large saturation stain of suspected blood and possibly motor oil. Surrounding this were drops of blood and motor oil on the perimeter. The saturation stain was large, covering a two-by-two-foot area. "The saturation stain was sufficiently large enough to suggest that the bleeding individual remained at that location for a period of time before being moved," Wilgus noted.

In addition to the blood and motor oil, Wilgus noticed that bleach appeared to have been used on some areas of the carpet. Cleaning bottles left nearby suggested that the attacker had attempted to clean up or hide the blood on the carpet but had eventually given up. The area of the carpeting with the saturation stain was cut out and collected as evidence.

Wilgus also noted several spatter stains on the west wall of the living room. Their height ranged from forty-five inches to six feet above the floor, and stretched across the wall for about forty-eight inches.

Leading from the large saturation stain on the living room carpet was a swipe pattern consistent with an object, such as a body, being dragged. This pattern led from the saturation stain, down the hallway, to the entrance of the bathroom.

Moving on to Tina's bedroom, Wilgus found another saturation stain of blood covered over by motor oil, on the carpet. Wilgus noted, "The saturation stain was large enough to suggest that the bleeding individual remained at the location for a period of time before being moved." The wording was the same for this next supposed victim as it had been for a supposed victim in the front room. This carpeting was also cut out and collected as evidence.

In this bedroom there was also a comforter with a blood saturation stain, again covered over by motor oil. It was found lying on the floor near the northeast corner of the bed. An apparent impact pattern was spattered on the dresser and closet doors of the bedroom. The pattern radiated from the south to the north, and originated somewhere near the nightstand between the dresser and bed.

A swipe pattern consistent with a bloodstained object being dragged and motor oil being poured over the swipe stain led from the bedroom, down the hallway and into the bathroom.

In the hallway the transfer pattern and swipe patterns were consistent with bloodstained fabric, most likely from a gloved hand, coming in contact with the wall. The pattern was about fifty-eight inches above the floor.

In Sarah's bedroom Wilgus found yet another large saturation stain. From the saturation stain a swipe pattern led through the bedroom, down the hallway, to the bathroom. This too was consistent with an object being dragged, perhaps a body. And on the west side of the swipe pattern, there were shoe prints consistent with tennis shoes, left in motor oil. These may well have been impressions left by an assailant.

On the north wall of Sarah's bedroom, an impact pattern covered one wall and curtain. The pattern radiated from west to east, and the impact occurred close to the wall, approximately twenty to forty inches above the floor. On Sarah's bedroom door, someone had left blood transfer patterns on the exterior of the door.

It was in the bathroom, however, where Wilgus discovered the most bloodstains in various forms. "The bathtub and shower walls of the main bathroom on the first floor of the home exhibited a large amount of blood," he reported. "The stains consisted of transfer patterns and spatter stains. A significant amount of the blood appeared to be altered by water. Intermixed within the patterns were pieces of apparent body fat. On the top edges of the tub and the toilet, which was also blood covered, were apparent fabric prints in blood."

Given the scope of all these bloodstains and spatter, it would take Special Agent Wilgus and later BCI&I Special Agent Daniel Winterich, who joined him, a great deal of time to tabulate and categorize every stain.

Moving on, Wilgus noted on the east wall of the stairwell to the basement, a spatter stain above the third step from the bottom of the stairs. This blood was not altered or diluted with anything.

At the bottom of the basement stairs, however, on the vinyl floor, there were circular drops of blood that were altered or diluted. And near the Jeep in the garage were blood drops with "spines" that indicated that the blood drop had a lateral movement toward the west wall of the garage. Spines on blood drops generally notated some kind of movement by an individual.

Other blood drops were found here and there on the garage floor. Some had been altered or diluted, and others had not. On the inside of the garage door was a blood transfer pattern where it appeared that someone's gloved hand had made the transfer.

One of Wilgus's most important findings was the shoe-print patterns that had been left, in blood, motor oil or a combination of both, throughout the house. One set of patterns was very distinctive: the prints were shaped like "lobster claws." Wilgus noted, "The pattern was repetitive and consistent in size and shape. Believing they were from a lug of a shoe or boot, we identified some of the most well-defined patterns and cut them from the carpeting." These prints were a key piece of evidence because they might have come from the assailant's shoe or boot.

The best of these patterns was found near the doorway of the northwest bedroom and in the hallway just outside that bedroom door. In addition to these shoe prints, there were also similar shoe prints left in blood near the toilet of the main bathroom. The pattern of the sole appeared to have solid circles connected by a line. These shoe prints were photographed, and the agents even collected the actual vinyl flooring near the toilet as evidence.

Using magnetic fingerprint powder, Wilgus and Winterich discovered even more of this distinctive shoe pattern leading from the bathroom to the garage. From the master bedroom the agents collected and catalogued an acetate sheet with hair on it, as well as bloodstained bedding and comforters, and a shoe box. From Sarah's room the agents lifted a shoe impression on the carpet, unknown tissue found on a toy bear, and what looked to be an impression left by the perpetrator in some blood.

A shoe print also thought to be from the perpetrator was found in the hallway, and cloth gloves were found in the living room. The agents surmised that the perpetrator may have used these gloves since there were indications of blood and other material on them.

In another of the shoe impressions, the agents were able to discern the brand name "Airwalk." It was from a size seven-and-a-half shoe. A further search of the house revealed that all the women's shoes in the master bed-

room closet were size eight. All the shoes in Sarah's
closet were size seven and a half. It was deduced that the
shoe impression came from Sarah.

One of the agents wrote in his report, "Due to the
impressions being in the oil-like substance, it was believed that the wearer of the shoes was upright and walking through the crime scene, stepped in the oil and
then walked onto the linoleum floor." In other words, it
looked as if the girl in the residence, Sarah Maynard, had
not been killed there but had instead walked on the linoleum surface to the garage area. Just what happened to
her after that, however, they did not know. But this was
a very important bit of information—there was a possibility she was still alive.

A second person's shoe-impression design was also revealed as a result of the magnetic fingerprint powder
being applied to the linoleum floor. This caused a problem. Had there been a second assailant in the house, or
had that impression been left by one of the detectives
who had been in the house earlier in the day? Or could it
have even been from Valerie Haythorn, who'd first entered the house? This second "suspect" shoe impression
was covered with craft paper to preserve it until all of the
KCSO officers' shoes, and Valerie Haythorn's, could be
examined and ruled out.

In addition to the many, many bloodstains covering
the bathroom, especially around the toilet and tub, the
detectives found and seized a Nokia cell phone and case
from the bathroom floor. There were also gloves found in
the bathroom sink as well as a box of trash bags. This was

a second set of gloves in addition to the pair already found. These gloves were cloth as well. Other items in the bathroom included Clorox bathroom cleaner, a bottle of Shout left in the bathroom sink, and Solutions cleaner, as well as four toothbrushes. Two more partial shoe impressions were lifted from the bathroom floor. Shoe impressions were also lifted near the front door and near the top of the stairs.

The agents took swabs from all over the house in hopes of picking up fingerprints and other key evidence. These included swabs from the bathroom sink handles, the basement doorknob, two Samsung cell phones, the hallway wall, the spatter on Sarah's bedroom wall, and the side of the bathtub.

A break in the processing came for Agents Winterich and Wilgus at around 9:45 PM. They, along with Detective Sergeant Brown, went up the street on Magers Drive to check on a tip about Stephanie Sprang's boyfriend Ronald Metcalf having recently dug a hole in their yard.

From a neighbor's yard, all three men saw a freshly dug area that was approximately twelve inches in diameter. Winterich noted, "Metcalf was interviewed about the hole and stated [that one of the children's] pet rabbit had died and that he buried it in a cardboard box. He completed a written consent form, and Agent Wilgus and I dug up the box and confirmed that it was a rabbit. We cleared, returned back to the crime scene, and continued to assist with the crime scene investigation."

Stephanie's Jeep Cherokee, which had been found in Tina's garage, was also thoroughly searched and catalogued, including swabs from stains on the edge of the front seat, rear passenger seat, passenger-side rocker panel and doorknobs. It was the garage itself, however, that gave up some of the most important clues yet.

The first was a bloody shoe impression in the garage that was determined to have most likely *not* come from the perpetrator. It was small in size and probably the shoe imprint of a child. The investigators wondered whether this shoe imprint had been left there by Kody or by Sarah; if so, one of them might still be alive.

The second clue was a sudden flash of good police work. Detective David Light noted that, "In the garage, officers located a Walmart bag that contained several tarps and an opened bag of 55 gallon heavy duty trash bags." The detectives surmised that the perpetrator might've brought those items himself to the crime scene. Judging by the amount of blood in the bathroom, especially in the bathtub, the detectives posited that the perpetrator might have carved up one or more bodies in the bathtub and then placed the body parts within the heavy trash bags. Then he might have driven away with the body-filled bags to some unknown location, while leaving the unused trash bags behind in the garage.

THIRTEEN

In the Dark

All during November 10 and most of November 11, Larry Maynard had no idea that anything was amiss with his ex-wife, Tina, or their children, Sarah and Kody. He and his family lived south of Columbus, more than fifty miles away from all the activity in Knox County.

Larry's first indication that something was wrong was when he received a phone call from Tina's boyfriend, Greg Borders. The phone call came in on a number he rarely gave out, one he had not given to Greg, so hearing Greg's voice on the line threw Larry for a loop. Besides, Larry and Greg had not exactly gotten along over the years.

Larry said later, "Greg asked me where Tina and the kids were. I wondered, 'Why in the hell is he asking me? He's the one who should know where they are.' Then I asked him how he got this number. He said he found it on a Rolodex. He said a few more things and then hung up. I immediately became concerned, and wondered once again why he was the one who didn't know where they were. After all, they were living in his house!"

Larry turned on the local news and was stunned to see a report of four people missing in Knox County from the Apple Valley area. That was of course where Tina, Sarah and Kody lived; Larry didn't know about Stephanie Sprang. As of that point, not one police officer had contacted him. Larry was totally in the dark as to what was happening except for the few details on the television news. But Larry Maynard's sleepless nights were just beginning.

There were sleepless nights for Tina's brothers as well. Tracy Herrmann, who was married to Tina's brother Jason, later said, "It began for us when Jason got a phone call that there was caution tape surrounding Tina's house. I remember waiting until midnight and praying that whatever happened was just a misunderstanding. Jason came home and said he knew something was very wrong due to all of the law enforcement that were present."

The lack of information being dispensed by the police only added to Jason's and Tracy's anxiety. Just like Larry Maynard, they were very much in the dark about the situation concerning Tina, Sarah and Kody. And they didn't yet know that Stephanie was missing too.

* * *

In Knox County, the lockdown on the Kenyon College campus was finally lifted at 7:00 AM on November 12. Anxiety remained high there, however, and Mark Ellis, spokesman for the college, related, "There is still concern and our thoughts are with the families." The students on campus breathed a sigh of relief, but still they were on edge. Why had the missing person's vehicle ended up so close to the college? Was a student on campus involved with whatever was going on? Or even a faculty member?

An initial article in the *Mount Vernon News* about the missing people was very brief, noting simply that KCSO detectives had searched Tina Herrmann's residence on King Beach Drive and found a "substantial amount" of blood there. The article also reported that the Ohio State Highway Patrol (OSHP) had offered their services to KCSO and that the request had been accepted.

Sergeant Gary Lewis of OSHP told the reporter that OSHP's role in the investigation would be one of support, explaining, "We have use of a FLIR, which is a heat thermal imaging instrument used from a helicopter. It is not uncommon for us to use this equipment in these situations."

The FLIR, or forward-looking infrared radar, would be used from the helicopter to conduct a search from the air, and the information gathered would be coordinated with ground crews, as well as with KCSO. A trunking system would allow communications between all parties with no outside interference. In other words, no one would be able to hack into the conversations, as could happen with someone using a police scanner to scan normal police-radio traffic. This was important in case the perpetrator was trying to listen in on such calls.

November 12, Larry Maynard could no longer stand the suspense of not knowing what was happening, and he and his wife decided to travel the fifty-plus miles to the Knox County Sheriff's Office in Mount Vernon. At this point Larry had very little information other than what Greg had said in their phone conversation and what he'd seen on the television news.

After arriving at the sheriff's station, Larry explained to the person at the front-desk window who he was and why he had come and was then led back to a conference room. He was accompanied by his wife, Tracy, and another couple, friends who'd come along to offer moral support. There, they met with a detective and began to answer some questions about Tina, Sarah and Kody. "All of it was very general, just getting background information," Larry said later. "The detective did not have a lot to say about what the sheriff's office was doing, other than it was a missing persons' case. Then just before we were about ready to leave, the detective told me, 'Larry, we need to talk to you alone.'

"I was escorted back into what I'd call an investigation room. There was a large mirror on one wall, and I figured some other detective was behind that mirror, watching what was going on. Two detectives started asking me questions. The questions were like, when was the last time I'd seen Tina, Kody or Sarah. They asked how my relationship was with Tina. I said that we got along and were civil to each other. There were times when she'd call me if the kids were acting up and needed talking to. I'd say things to Kody or Sarah like, 'You can't act that way. You have to treat your mom with respect.' Things like that.

"They asked about the house, and their ears really perked up when I mentioned the garage door. They wanted to know why I mentioned something like that. I said I knew that it was broken and would not close all the way. The reason I knew that was because Tina had called me one time and said that Greg had broken it. He'd been angry or something and broken the garage door.

"The detectives asked me where I'd been on Tuesday and Wednesday, and I told them. When it was all over they walked me out of the room, and one of them said to me, 'Sorry we had to do that, Larry, but we had to ask you those questions.' I knew they were checking me out and that was their job. All I wanted them to do was find Tina, Sarah and Kody.

"On the way out to our car in the parking lot, I thought I saw Greg Borders sitting in a vehicle there in the parking lot. He was in the passenger seat, and I think his uncle was in the driver's seat. I wondered what he was doing there."

Greg Borders was indeed there, and detectives also interviewed him. Greg explained that he, Tina, Sarah and Kody lived together at the crime scene address on King Beach Drive. Greg said that both he and Tina had a mortgage on the residence, though he added that, "Lately our relationship has not been the best." He said that for the last few days he had been staying at a friend's house, because he'd gone golfing out of town and it was far from Apple Valley. He'd stayed overnight at his friend's house on November 10, golfed the next day and hadn't known anything was wrong at home until he'd gotten a call from his uncle, who later told reporters, "I went past the house and saw the yellow tape. I called Greg, and he was on his way back. He'd been out golfing, [which was of course on November 11]."

Later that day, November 12th, WBNS News from Columbus spoke with Greg Borders. According to the news account, "Borders said the couple was having trouble, but said he knows nothing and has done nothing wrong. He said he last saw Herrmann and her children around 4:00 AM Wednesday, before he left for work at a Target distribution center in West Jefferson. He received a message from her at 11:00 AM. Borders said that was the last time he heard from her."

WBNS News then spoke with Larry Maynard, and reported, "Larry Maynard said he is not so sure [about Greg Borders' involvement]. Larry related, 'The boyfriend, the live-in boyfriend, Greg—I don't believe anything he says. My kids are my world. It's like somebody ripped the heart out of me. I don't want to believe that something has happened to them, but in my heart, I know something has happened to them.'"

Oddly, the local news stations were trying to get news out of Larry Maynard, even though he was still depending on *them* for updates. Despite his interview at the sheriff's office, that office was giving Larry very little information. On the one hand, he understood that—they had an investigation to do and didn't want anything they said to him to jeopardize that. On the other hand, it was very frustrating to be kept in the dark.

By now, even the national television news agencies were picking up on the story. ABC News reported, "A spokesman for the FBI Field Office in Cincinnati said the agency was aware of the incident but could not comment on whether it would cooperate with the investigation." And ABC News also broadcast a statement from Sheriff Barber that "the search of the home has revealed it to be in an unusual condition for a place where a woman and children lived." Barber did not elaborate on what that meant.

In the meantime, tips had started coming in. At first they were just a trickle, but soon they would become a flood. That trickle began on November 12th.

One was from a woman named Tammy R, who said, "I saw a male at an auction on Saturday at Horn Road. He was wearing a yellow sweatshirt and approximately five-feet, eleven inches. He had dark hair, facial hair and stood back away from the crowd smoking. And on this same day I saw rolling black smoke coming from an area of the second barn on a property nearby. Like someone was burning a tire. No one was supposed to be there. Then later at night I saw a flash of light that came through my living room. I got scared and went upstairs. There was pounding on that property for sale nearby, as if someone was working on it. It sounded like it was coming from one of the barns."

Another tip came in to KCSO about a bloody tarp out in some woods in the area. Detective Sergeant Brown and Agent Winterich, who had been processing the crime scene, went to the patch of woods off of Beaver Road. Winterich documented later, "The tarp was determined to be home wrap [typically used in construction projects], and it was located approximately fifty feet from the roadway. A reddish-brown stain was visible and it was presumptively tested for the presence of blood using the chemical Tetramethylbenzidine. A positive reaction occurred." But although there was certainly blood on the tarp, Winterich went on to say that "a HemDirect Hemoglobin test was then performed on the stain and this indicated that the blood was not human in origin."

One tipster, a woman named Patricia C, related, "My son called me and said Trisha [Stephanie's daughter] was looking for Stephanie. Said she has been missing since Wednesday the 10. I went to the Dairy Queen to see if her friend Tina had seen her. I found out that Tina was missing too. I talked to Tina's supervisor at work. We went to a rental where Tina and Stephanie went to look for a place to rent. No luck."

Soon there was another tip by a man named Brian K who contacted KCSO. Brian said, "As far as Stephanie's vehicle being found in Tina's garage, that is not unusual because she would put it there."

A tipster named Felicia W contacted KCSO on November 12 and related, "I last spoke to [Stephanie] on Sunday and she sounded fine. I was supposed to call her back Monday evening, but didn't get a chance. She would never leave her home and kids."

By now the FBI was involved, and the lead agent on the case was Special Agent Harry Trombitas of the Columbus, Ohio, office. His main activity on November 12 was interviewing people who lived close to the scene of the crime. Trombitas contacted neighbors on Magers Road and noted that although they were very cooperative, none of them had seen anything or heard anything suspicious before or during the time the crime was thought to have happened.

Trombitas then contacted Mike Sprang, Stephanie's ex-husband. Mike was also cooperative and said that he and Stephanie had been married for three years, but there had been "issues between them" and they got a divorce. Mike said that he had no animosity toward Stephanie and hadn't seen her recently. He was worried about her disappearance.

Next on the list were Ron Metcalf, Stephanie's boyfriend, and Michael Kupiec, her older son, both of whom lived with Stephanie on Magers Road. Ron was noted as being "cooperative" and stated that Stephanie had stayed home on Tuesday night into Wednesday morning, November 10, and said that they had had coffee together around 6:00 AM. Trish, Stephanie's daughter, was in the house as well, but she was still asleep in the morning hours.

Ron said that he'd left for his job at Rolls Royce Energy Systems in Mount Vernon at 6:30 AM and that everything was fine with Stephanie at that time. Around 12:26 PM, he received a text from Stephanie that indicated she was "in town."

Ron had been having a problem with a credit card account and he was having Stephanie help him with it. She called him on his cell phone at 12:46 PM to tell him that she didn't have that account number and couldn't help him at present. The call lasted four minutes and seventeen seconds. Ron told Agent Trombitas that was the last he'd heard from Stephanie.

Ron also told Trombitas that he'd heard Stephanie had called a friend of hers named Forrest Frazee at 12:17 PM that same day. Forrest had not answered, and apparently Stephanie hadn't left a message. Forrest thought this was unusual, because Stephanie had only texted him in the past and generally did not talk to him on the phone. Ron had gotten all this information secondhand from a person who knew Frazee.

Ron then told Trombitas that he'd heard that Stephanie and Tina had planned to go to a tanning salon in Mount Vernon around noon on November 11. Ron didn't know if that had occurred or not. And he'd also heard they might be going out to look for a place for Tina in the afternoon. Ron added that he returned home at his usual time of 4:00 PM and was surprised when Stephanie was not there. It was very unusual because as

Ron put it, "She was always there to greet her kids when they got off the school bus."

Ron was surprised enough that he texted Stephanie's cell phone with a message, "What's up?" He then got an indication later that the message was "unread," and assumed that the battery in her cell phone had died.

Agent Trombitas noted in his report, "Metcalf stated that he was aware that Tina and her boyfriend, Greg Borders, had issues, but did not elaborate."

Stephanie's twenty-year-old son, Michael Kupiec was very cooperative and concerned about the welfare of his mother. Michael said he'd received a phone call Thursday morning from his sister, Trisha, who told him, "Mom's missing!"

Michael headed home and kept trying to reach his mom on her cell phone, but to no avail. Later in the day he got a call from Tina Herrmann's boyfriend, Greg Borders, but he missed that call; when he called Greg back, Greg told Michael that he'd been out playing golf with friends, but said that Stephanie and Tina were both missing, and that Tina's manager had gone into the house and contacted the sheriff's office. Greg told him that he'd given the police permission to enter the house, which they had. Greg went on to explain that the police had apparently found a lot of blood there, and that they'd then told him they needed to get a search warrant before proceeding.

Michael was visibly upset, and he told Agent Trombitas that Trombitas was the first law enforcement officer who had contacted him. Michael didn't understand why the sheriff's office hadn't contacted him yet, and he was completely in the dark about what had happened to his mother. He was just as in the dark about what was going on as Larry Maynard.

It was, of course, important for Special Agents Wilgus and Winterich of BCI&I to draw some kind of conclusion regarding the various bloodstains in Tina Herrmann's residence. From their conclusions, other investigators could get a better idea of what they were dealing with. To this end, the blood specialists made a list of six points.

First was that three individual saturation stains and their associated spatter stains were consistent with three of the four missing persons having been assaulted, resulting in significant blood loss in the house.

Second was that the three swipe patterns leading from the saturation stains to the bathtub—in conjunction with the amount of blood, tissue and fat deposits found in the bathtub itself—indicated the possibility of dismemberment or some other major injury to some or all of the missing persons.

Third was that the altered bloodstains in the bathtub, on the vinyl floor at the front door and at the bottom of the steps leading into the garage indicated some movement of the missing persons after contact with water or other altering substances.

Fourth was that the presence of bleached carpeting, motor oil and wipe patterns all indicated an attempt to alter, hide, remove or cover the bloodstains.

Fifth was that the presence of nonaltered, passive drops of blood in separate parts of the house indicated the possibility of an individual having been cut or injured. In addition to the three individuals who had sustained a major bleeding event and/or dismemberment, there was a different outcome for one individual. Either the perpetrator or the fourth victim had been merely cut during the assault.

And finally, the sixth point was that the lack of fingerprint or palm-print ridge detail in blood and the presence of fabric patterns in blood indicated that the assailant had probably been wearing gloves at the time of the bloodletting events.

BCI&I Special Agent Joe Dietz worked well into the late-night hours of November 12, like many other law enforcement officers that day. He noted later, "Jeremy Biggs voluntarily came to the Knox County Sheriff's Office and was interviewed by me. Also present for the interview was Special Agent Rick Wozniak of the Federal Bureau of Investigation. Jeremy Biggs had sold the Jeep to Stephanie and still had his name on the Department of Vehicles registration form.

"Biggs stated that he and Stephanie Sprang [had been] best friends for three years but had never really dated. Biggs stated he was last in contact with Sprang at 12:10 PM on Wednesday, November 10th, while he was at work. Biggs said he spoke to Sprang on the phone at that time and she was actually at his house doing schoolwork on his computer." Just what classes she may have been taking or why she was doing schoolwork he didn't say.

"Biggs added that Sprang cleaned his house once a week as a part time job. Biggs also said that the Jeep Cherokee that Sprang drove was in his name as a result of it having been bought shortly after Sprang had a DUI arrest. Biggs said although Sprang paid for the vehicle, it could not be put in her name for insurance purposes.

"Biggs said that he was at work all day on Wednesday and that he was in a sales meeting most of the day with several people at work. [His general manager] could account for his being there on November 10." November 10 was the day that Tina, Sarah, Kody and Stephanie disappeared.

Agent Dietz later followed up on Jeremy Biggs's story, and the general manager at the Mount Vernon Jeld-Wen Windows and Doors facility were Jeremy worked confirmed it, saying that Jeremy had come to work around 8:00 AM and left around 5:00 PM that day.

The manager also added that Jeremy had often referred to Stephanie Sprang as his "best friend."

FOURTEEN

"An Unusual Amount of Blood"

By Saturday, November 13, 2010, a reporter contacted East Middle School, which both Sarah and Kody Maynard attended. East Knox Schools Superintendent Matthew Caputo confirmed that the children had been in school on Wednesday, November 10, but not on November 11. In fact, the school had made a courtesy call on that same day to see if the children were all right. They'd received no response.

Caputo said that KCSO was taking care of matters now, so he couldn't say much more. He did add, however, that plans were in place if a "crisis" had occurred. "We have procedures we follow to ensure we are taking care of the needs of the kids. If a student is bothered by something, we are going to have a set of ears to listen to them and help them to be able to get through whatever it is. We also have some local folks who we can call on, youth ministers and such."

After all of Matthew Hoffman's exertions over the last few days, he finally felt safe enough to spend more time with the girl in his house. There was no doubt in his mind that she was pretty. She was very young, but that didn't matter to him. Since she was tied up, she'd have to go along with whatever he wanted.

Sarah had been lying on a bed of leaves that Hoffman had constructed for her in the dark basement. She felt distressed and ashamed that she had wet herself while tied up there, but there was nothing she could do about it. He hadn't let her use the bathroom when she needed to. At least he'd put gloves on her hands; otherwise, the cold dank basement might have been unbearable.

Suddenly the man was back downstairs and asking her to do something. At first she didn't understand what it was he was asking, but then it became all too plain. He said some things to her that disgusted her, but she knew this was one more thing that she'd have to endure if she wanted to stay alive.

More than fifty miles away, Larry and his family felt like they were in a bunker of their own. Media vans and reporters surrounded the house. Larry's mind wandered between anger, hope and despair. He knew that the longer this ordeal went on, the less likely it was that there would be a good ending to all of it. Tracy brought out food for him to eat, but he barely touched it. His stomach was tied in knots and no food was appealing to him. He wondered what to tell AJ. What do you tell a boy that young about a situation like this?

Tina's brother Bill was suffering through the same emotions as Larry. His girlfriend, Lisa Robey, later related, "I remember one night after leaving the police station, we had stopped at a restaurant. We hadn't eaten in days, and still were not hungry, but we knew we needed to eat. While sitting at a table, I started looking at the people around me. While I was looking, I remember thinking, 'What's wrong with everyone? Why are they happy? Why are they laughing? Why are they complaining about mashed potatoes? Don't they know what just happened? Don't they know that our world has stopped?' For some reason, I had thought that just because our lives stopped, everyone else's should have also.

"That's not the way the world works. You sometimes see and hear of the tragic stories on TV, and naturally feel sorry for the families, but never think it would happen to your family, or someone that you know. There were endless trips to Mount Vernon. Numerous phone calls from family and friends wanting answers, in which we had no answers to give."

* * *

On November 13, Lieutenant Gary Rohler and Detective Doug Turpen interviewed Alexa Leasure at the sheriff's office. Alexa was a friend and coworker of Tina's from Dairy Queen. Alexa explained to the officers that Tina had been having relationship problems with Greg Borders, and that Tina was in the process of finding a new place to rent. Tina, Sarah and Kody were going to move out of the King Beach Drive residence.

Next on the list of people the officers talked to was Valerie Haythorn, who took them again through the story about her concern for Tina, and how she'd decided to enter the residence on King Beach Drive. Valerie reiterated that once she saw blood, she'd exited quickly and called the sheriff's office.

Both Lieutenant Rohler and Detective Turpen followed Valerie to her own house after the interview and collected the pair of shoes she had been wearing when she entered Tina's home. These shoes were taken as evidence in the case, so that the forensics team could try to decipher any footprints Valerie might have left in Tina's home from those left by the assailant.

Lieutenant Rohler and Detective Turpen went to Stephanie Sprang's residence on Magers Road and were given consent to search and seize items that belonged to Stephanie. These included her computer, three toothbrushes, a yellow bag with various papers inside and several other items including jewelry, such as a ring with a missing stone. Stephanie's stepfather's truck was also searched for items that might have belonged to her.

* * *

Special Agent Joe Dietz of BCI&I was very busy on November 13. Around 11:00 AM he arrived at the Target Distribution Center in West Jefferson, Ohio, where Greg Borders worked, and met with Chris Grieser, the logistics senior group leader at that location, to verify Greg Borders's presence at work on Wednesday, November 10.

Chris told Agent Dietz that the facility was very secure, that each employee had to scan ID cards at various security points, and that once inside the facility, employees were not allowed to leave until the end of their shifts. Chris also told Dietz about security cameras at all entrance and exit points of the building, and agreed to contact the personnel/human resources supervisor and have them come in to access the video and records on Greg Borders.

While waiting for the video evidence to be obtained, Dietz went to the Urbana, Ohio, residence of Patrick Sandy, one of Greg's coworkers at the Target Distribution Center, to meet with him and his wife. Patrick told Dietz that on Monday, November 8, he and Greg had indeed made plans to go golfing on Thursday, November 11.

Patrick related that he'd made online reservations to play at the Tree Links in Bellefontaine, Ohio, and that because of its distance away, he'd invited Greg to stay overnight at his house on Wednesday, November 10. Patrick said that Greg had arrived around 5:15 PM that night and had called earlier from a Speedway store to discuss what beer he should pick up and bring over. According to Patrick's cell phone log, that call had been placed at 4:45 PM. Patrick said that after Greg arrived, they'd watched TV until around 11:30 PM, and then the next morning, they'd gotten up and went to play golf as planned.

Patrick confirmed that he and Greg were together playing golf at Tree Links for most of the day that Thursday, November 11. They'd been joined by another friend, Nadeem Siddiqui, who was a former Target employee. Patrick stated that he recalled Greg getting a cell phone call around noon from his mother, who told him that Tina had not gone to work the day before and was missing. It was not apparent to Greg or Patrick at the time why Greg's mom would know this fact. Greg told Patrick that he thought Tina had taken the day off work. According to Patrick, Greg did not know at that point that Sarah and Kody had also not shown up for school that day. All three men continued playing golf until around 3:00 or 3:30 PM, and then Greg left the golf course to return home. It was before he reached home on King Beach Drive that his uncle contacted him.

Based on Patrick's information, Agent Dietz went to the Speedway store in Urbana from which Greg had reportedly called Patrick, and talked to the assistant manager, who made him a CD of the store videotape from November 10 that covered 4:00 to 6:00 PM. Dietz reviewed the tape, which confirmed that Greg Borders had been there buying beer at 4:45 PM.

Around 12:45 PM November 13, Agent Dietz went

back to the Target Distribution Center and met again with Chris Grieser. Chris told him that a check of records, including card scans and videos, showed Greg Borders entering the facility at 5:45 AM on November 10 and leaving at 4:05 PM that same day. Chris said that he spoke with the area manager who'd supervised Greg on November 10, and the manager recalled that Greg had been at work throughout that day.

By now news agencies out of the Mount Vernon area were interested in the developing story, noting the law enforcement personnel guarding the perimeter of Tina Herrmann's house and the investigators coming and going, some of them wearing scrubs, gloves and protective booties.

A reporter from the *Columbus Dispatch* was able to talk to Greg Borders in front of the house on King Beach Drive. He told him, "I have a thousand things running through my head and I want some answers." Greg went on to say that he and Tina had recently broken up, but that they, along with her children, were all still sharing the house they'd lived in since 2007. He'd heard through others that on the day they disappeared, Tina and Stephanie Sprang had planned to go out to look at some apartments and houses in the area.

Greg went on to recount how he had been out of town golfing on November 11 and the first he'd known anything was wrong was when his uncle told him that there was police activity at his residence.

Reporters were also able to contact Sarah and Kody's father, Larry Maynard. He said, "It's like somebody ripped my heart out while it's still beating. You have this kind of thing on TV all the time, but it's never your family. I'm no dummy. I know the longer these things go on, the worse the chances. Sarah is a bubbly child and a star athlete on the softball team. Kody is quieter and a good student who's always on the honor roll."

Later that day, November 13th, Sheriff Barber held a press conference, an occurrence that would become routine over the coming days. He began by saying, "On behalf of the Knox County Sheriff's Office and the families of Stephanie and Tina, I'd like to thank you in the media for assisting us as far as the four of them being missing. The photographs [of the missing individuals] and things like that have been very helpful. We've received some good information—so we appreciate the participation of you folks.

"Any kind of information we receive, tips and other things, are being followed up by investigators. Evidence is continuing to be collected. BCI&I is not back yet, but will be later on today, processing Tina's truck, which was recovered near Kenyon College on Thursday evening. They're also processing the vehicle that belonged to Stephanie that was found in the garage at the scene.

"It is our hope that evidence obtained from both of these vehicles, as well as evidence that has been and will continue to be collected from the house, will lead to more information as to their disappearance.

"We are asking people to keep a guarded but optimistic attitude about how the case is going to unfold. We would constantly ask that everyone, not just in Knox County, but in Ohio—well, they [the missing] do have friends and family outside of Knox County—we would ask that on behalf of them and their families we all keep them in our thoughts and prayers and hope for a positive outcome.

"What is taking place and will continue to take place today is that the aircraft that you see overhead are from the Ohio State Highway Patrol's aviation unit. They are flying over this area, and they have infrared equipment and are checking some areas. We also have officers on quad runners searching some areas around here.

"In the area around Gambier, there have been some citizen volunteers. They thoroughly searched some areas on Thursday and Friday. We do hope these folks, if they do come across something that looks unusual, they will stay back away from it and notify the sheriff's office immediately.

"If anyone sees something unusual or has any information about Sarah, Tina, Kody or Stephanie, call the Knox County Sheriff's Office. Our detectives would also like to have contact with anyone who may have had contact with any of the four of them any time on Wednesday.

"We have talked to a lot of people that have had contact with them [before Wednesday]. Students at the East

Knox schools where Sarah and Kody go to school. Folks like that. What we're trying to do is try and establish a timeline and try to find out if there was anything unusual about the four of them. If they had any concerns about family issues and things like that."

Sheriff Barber then opened the floor to questions from the media. One reporter asked, "Are the airplanes, helicopters and people on four-runners looking for anything specific?"

Barber replied, "We're looking for anything or anyone that may have gone from Tina's house away from the scene."

Reporters asked if the investigators were searching nearby lakes. Sheriff Barber answered, "Yes, we have watercraft out today. And as potentially tragic as this week has been, we have been blessed with good weather. That has definitely improved our chances of locating evidence and locating those four people."

He said they were searching Apple Valley Lake and that investigators from the Ohio Department of Natural Resources had gone around the lake with scent dogs, though the dogs had not picked up any indications that the missing people had been there. Barber added that the lake was so large, it would be a waste of time to just send divers out on a random search.

Another reporter queried, "Is it still just a missing person case?"

Barber answered that it was, and in response to a question about whether people in general should be concerned, he said that, no, "people should just use common sense as far as their children go and personal safety."

Another reporter asked, "Just so we get this right. You are not saying at this point that you think these four are dead?"

Barber replied, "Not at this time, no."

Someone wanted to know if there had been any activity on any of the missing people's credit cards. Barber said there hadn't been, and added, "We're checking those kinds of things. Bank accounts, cell phones, text messages. We are utilizing the FBI in doing a lot of analysis for us. We've also joined forces with the Central Ohio Child Abduction Response Team, which includes Franklin and Delaware County detectives. They were here most of yesterday."

One reporter wanted to know more about the blood that had been found in the residence, how much of it there was and where exactly it had been located.

Sheriff Barber declined to go into specifics, citing investigative reasons, but noted that "there was an unusual amount of blood in that house. The one thing I can say is, it was not from someone stubbing their toe or cutting their finger while peeling an apple."

"It's not like an ax murder or anything like that, right?" the reporter asked.

"No," Barber said.

Though in truth, that wasn't a far-off description of events.

"How long will it be for BCI&I to analyze the

blood?" another reporter asked, and Barber responded that BCI&I was making it a priority case, but that it would take more than just a few days to do the analysis.

In response to "Any persons of interest surface at this time?" Barber said there were none as yet.

"You've talked to Greg, the boyfriend?" a reporter pressed.

"Yes, certainly."

"And he is not a suspect?"

"No, he is not."

A journalist commented, "Stephanie had three children, I believe. Do you know what is going on with them?"

Barber said, "Detectives have interviewed those family members. And they, like the rest of us, are brainstorming to try and figure out where Stephanie went."

"Are Stephanie's children in any kind of custody, like human services?"

"No. I think her youngest is nine, and there is a twenty-year-old son and seventeen-year-old daughter. They are not in custody of children's services or anything like that."

"You're getting a lot of help from the FBI and other agencies—can you tell us what the functions of your office is right now?"

Sheriff Barber responded, "We are the primary investigating agency. Obviously when you have a situation of this magnitude—I mean it's very unusual you would have four people go missing at the same time. We did ask for assistance. As far as the analysis of evidence and computer analysis, the FBI has those kinds of resources." Barber added, "I've never been afraid to ask for help. You know that the Knox County Sheriff's Office will participate with anyone it takes to get the case done."

The WBNS television station out of Columbus, Ohio, spoke with Larry Maynard again for a short time that day. Larry told a reporter, "Tina was searching for a new place to live." He added that Sarah and Kody had told him things that did not put Greg in the best light.

Greg Borders, who said of his relationship with Tina, "We were fairly civil. I mean, as civil as you can be living in the same house when you are split up. There were arguments every once in a while and disagreements, but I was still watching her kids at night when she went to work. I do think that something bad happened."

As to that part, Larry Maynard told the reporter, "I'm expecting the worst, but hoping for the best."

By now, some of Sarah's and Kody's friends had gotten involved. One of their friends, Morgan McCarthy, created a page on Facebook to coordinate volunteer search activities in the region. McCarthy told a reporter, "I'm hoping that they find them and they are safe and Kody and Sarah are back in school soon." By that night, more than six hundred people had joined the group page, which became a repository for messages and prayers. One of them was from Rebecca Cook, who wrote, "I'm hoping that someone will see the missing people at a gas station where they might be on vacation or something, and they say, 'Hey, people are looking for you.'"

Though Larry Maynard hoped that would happen, deep down he knew it was a very slim possibility.

FIFTEEN

A Huge Break

On November 13, 2010, Captain David Shaffer contacted Walmart in Mount Vernon to cross-reference purchases of the tarps and fifty-five-gallon heavy-duty trash
bags found in Tina Herrmann's garage. A woman from
customer service was able to locate the purchase of a tarp
with the same bar code and a purchase date and bar code
on the trash bags. The purchase had occurred just after
midnight on November 11, 2010. The only problem was
that the person who had bought the items had done so
with cash, not a credit or debit card.

To try and identify the person who had bought the
items, BCI&I Special Agent Joe Dietz and Detective David Light went to Walmart to request that the
store provide them with a video of purchases made
around the given time frame. They spoke with Jared

Scoles of the store's security department, telling him that they needed the video immediately.

Dietz noted in his own report that he obtained a copy of the receipt for the transaction, and by comparing the product codes on the receipt with items on the shelf, and relaying that information to Special Agent Daniel Winterich at the crime scene, was able to determine that the items recovered at the crime scene exactly matched the items purchased at Walmart. Dietz noted that in addition to the garbage bags listed on the receipt, tarps, a turkey sandwich and T-shirt had also been purchased during the same transaction.

Scoles provided a video for the two investigators. One person on the footage soon caught their attention: a white male who exited the store with a purchased tarp and garbage bags. He looked to be between twenty-five and forty years of age, and was wearing eyeglasses and a camouflage shirt. He had brown hair with a partially receding hairline. They could see on the security cameras that the man crossed the parking lot and got into a small silver-colored car, then drove out of the parking lot eastward in the direction of Apple Valley.

Scoles told the officers that he thought the car looked like a Toyota Yaris. The officers uploaded photos of a Toyota Yaris from the Internet and agreed that the silver car in the video matched that description.

This was a huge break. Officers began researching all male owners of Toyota Yaris's in Knox County. Special Agent Dietz and Lieutenant Gary Rohler checked the Ohio Law Enforcement Gateway system for owners of silver Toyota Yaris vehicles in Knox County. Rohler quickly pulled up one image that looked a great deal like the man on the videotape. The man was named Matthew J. Hoffman, and he had renewed his driver's license on October 26, only sixteen days previously. Incredibly, when Hoffman had his driver's license photo taken, he was wearing the same kind of camouflage shirt as the man on the Walmart videotape. While the new driver's license photo did not show Matthew Hoffman with glasses, earlier driver's license photos did.

Agent Dietz checked the Knox County Auditor website, looking for Hoffman's current address. He found two possibilities: the first listed was the 3000 block of Apple Valley Drive, within walking distance of King Beach Road, and the other location was 49 Columbus Road in Mount Vernon.

Over at Matthew Hoffman's house, Sarah lay alone on her bed of leaves. After forcing her to do things that disgusted her, he left her alone. It was dark, cold and damp down there, and her sense of time had almost evaporated by now. In fact, it was so dark down there, she could not tell night from day. She had no idea of all the frenzied police activity going on all around the area.

At least the man wasn't with her now. She had done what he wanted, and he'd left for some other part of the house. She was always cold, even though she was bundled up and covered with blankets. She even had gloves on her hands, which he'd put on her. It didn't matter, though; she still shivered from the frigid temperatures down in the basement.

Her stomach growled from hunger. All she'd had to eat since being kidnapped was a few mouthfuls of cereal with spoiled milk. She constantly thought of food, but was determined not to eat the squirrels he had offered her. She thought of daylight. But most of all, she thought of freedom.

At one point, the man gave her a dictionary and told her to look up the word "ransom." She did so and found out what it meant. Then he told her he might let her go by Christmas. He never explained exactly what he meant, but she didn't believe him in this regard anyway.

Sarah said later, "Even after he told me about the ransom, sometimes I thought he would kill me anyway, just so that it would be over with. It was scary."

He also told her now and again that he had someone watching the house. She was pretty sure he said "someone" as in one more person, rather than persons.

Things just kept getting better for the detectives. Lieutenant Rohler stated later, "As we were gathering additional information on Mr. Hoffman, we spoke with Deputy Aaron Phillips. Deputy Phillips was the officer who had located Tina Herrmann's F-150 pickup truck at the bike path in Gambier. Deputy Phillips indicated that he had confronted a white male sitting in a silver vehicle near the bike path at the same time that the F-150 truck was located. Deputy Phillips approached the white male and requested identification. Deputy Phillips ran the information through LEADS [Law Enforcement Agencies Data System] and the information returned to Matthew Hoffman."

Detective Sergeant Roger Brown looked up Matthew Hoffman in the KCSO computer system. The records showed that on Thursday, November 11 at around 6:55 PM, Deputy Aaron Phillips had made contact with Hoffman at the river access parking lot on Laymon Road, and that Hoffman had been sitting in a silver Yaris. Phillips was in the area because minutes earlier he'd noticed Tina Herrmann's Ford F-150 pickup parked at the Kokosing Gap Trail lot. The two parking lots were only two hundred yards apart.

And for the first time, Detective Sergeant Brown learned that Matthew Hoffman had told Phillips the reason he was sitting in his car was that he was waiting for his girlfriend, *Sarah,* to get off work at the Kenyon Inn. Brown also learned that Hoffman said he did not know Sarah's last name because they had just started dating. Phillips had told Hoffman the parking lot was closed after dark, and he had moved on.

Now Special Agent Dietz also discovered that Matthew Hoffman had been involved in a domestic violence issue with his then live-in girlfriend only a few weeks earlier, on October 24, 2010. This had occurred at the 49 Columbus Road location.

* * *

Because of all the information coming in, KCSO decided it was time to request a search warrant on Matthew Hoffman's residence at 49 Columbus Road. In the request, Detective David Light stated all the early facts about the search and seizure of items at King Beach Drive. He detailed how the record of the trash-bag purchase at Walmart had lead back to a video of a man exiting the store with a tarp and trash bags and getting into a silver Toyota Yaris in the store parking lot. Light stated that not only did the man in the video resemble the photo on Matthew Hoffman's driver's license, but he was also wearing the same kind of camouflage shirt as pictured in the driver's license photo.

Detective Light included the description of Deputy Aaron Phillips's interaction with a man in a silver Yaris parked near Tina Herrmann's pickup truck at the closed lot. During the encounter, Deputy Phillips had observed that the Yaris had a noticeable dent in it; so did the Yaris that had been videotaped leaving the Walmart parking lot.

Deputy Phillips would later say of these hectic minutes, "When the detectives got that information [about Matthew Hoffman], it was like [Ohio State University] just scored the winning touchdown. Guys were yelling and jumping up and down. Grabbing gear and sprinting out the door."

For all of these reasons, Detective Light wrote, "Your affiant has probable cause to believe that Matthew J. Hoffman purchased the trash bags and tarps at Wal-Mart, on November 11, 2010, and that he was in Tina Herrmann's residence where he left the trash bags and tarps and during the time of the criminal offenses alleged herein. Affiant has good cause to believe that Matthew J. Hoffman is dangerous and presents a risk of serious physical harm to law enforcement officers who will execute the search warrant."

Now Knox County Prosecutor John Thatcher became involved. He was contacted even though it was in the early morning hours of Sunday, November 14. Thatcher agreed there was enough probable cause for a warrant to be issued. He quickly set things in motion, despite the early hour. He said later, "I knew this was it. We had to go. I was already up and decided to come into the office instead of turning around and going back to bed until later that morning."

Thatcher said later that he knew time was of the essence. At least one of the missing people had walked in the garage area of the house on King Beach Road and might yet be alive. In fact, there was still a possibility that all four were still alive. Getting a search warrant as soon as possible was of grave importance.

Thatcher contacted Judge Paul Spurgeon, who read the request for the search warrant and signed it at 6:00 AM, November 14, 2010.

SIXTEEN

"A Dynamic Entry"

Very early on Sunday morning, November 14, 2010, Lieutenant Gary Rohler and Detective Sergeant Roger Brown began surveillance of Matthew Hoffman's residence at 49 Columbus Road. At that time, they discerned no activity in the residence or vehicles coming to or leaving the house.

Also early on November 14, Detective Craig Feeney of the Mount Vernon Police Department (MVPD) was contacted by Captain David Shaffer of KCSO. Shaffer told Feeney that KCSO wanted a Mount Vernon Police SWAT team to assist their office. Feeney passed this message on to Captain George Hartz of the MVPD, and a short time later Hartz told Feeney to start activating the SWAT team.

As the team was being put together, Feeney told all

the members to congregate at the Mount Vernon Police Department headquarters. One of these members was Sergeant Troy Glazier. As Glazier said later, "All available team members met at the police department and prepared our gear . . . Information at that time was that KCSO had developed leads to a possible suspect in the case of four missing persons. We geared up and went to the KCSO office for a briefing on the case. During the briefing, two locations were discussed where the suspect might be . . . We staged at Richert Trucking on Columbus Road until it could be determined the whereabouts of the suspect."

Around that same time, Detective Sergeant Roger Brown, Special Agent Joe Dietz, MVPD Captain George Hartz and KCSO Sergeant Jeff Jacobs went to the residence where Matt Hoffman's recent ex-girlfriend now lived. After brief questioning, she confirmed that Hoffman was living at the house on Columbus Road and not at his mother's home in Apple Valley. According to Detective Sergeant Brown, she also told them that Hoffman "normally did not park his vehicle at the residence due to the fear of it being repossessed."

Detective Feeney recalled, "Captain Shaffer went with our team and updated us on all current information coming in. Just prior to executing the warrant, Captain Shaffer received information that it was likely the suspect we were looking for was in the residence."

Glazier related, "With fresh information just developed that the suspect was most likely at the Columbus Road location, we headed that way. A marked KCSO unit was given a head start to get to the rear of the residence. The MVPD ESU van then proceeded to go do a 'dynamic' entry of the residence." A dynamic entry was one where a battering ram had to be used to break down a door.

"The ESU van pulled up to the front of the house, and we exited and stacked up at the front door. We were executing a no-knock search warrant, so we did not immediately announce our presence. Patrolman DeChant used a door ram to force entry, and I deployed a flash-bang distraction device inside the residence in the middle of the living room area. As soon as the distraction devices activated, the team entered the residence." "Entered" was hardly the right word—they stormed in like a hurricane.

"Patrolman Weiser and Detective Feeney encountered a male asleep on the couch in the living room. They began to give him verbal commands to show his hands, and he was not immediately compliant." (Whether Hoffman was being deliberately uncooperative or was merely groggy from lack of sleep was unclear).

Feeney stated, "We secured the male on the floor and identified him as the suspect. I escorted the male outside and re-entered the residence."

Glazier added, "Patrolman DeChant and I began to clear the area and located a stairway to the upper half of the house. Once we were comfortable that the downstairs area was cleared, we proceeded upstairs.

"The first door I came to upstairs was locked and I kicked the door in but did not locate any other persons upstairs. But we did locate what appeared to be a marijuana growing operation in one bedroom that was not active. We gave the all-clear upstairs and I had that team do a slowed-down secondary search of the upstairs. Patrolman DeChant and I located a hole that had been cut through the ceiling of a bedroom closet to gain access to the attic." The officers wanted to make sure no one was in the attic.

Glazier continued, "Patrolman [Tim] Arnold [of the Mount Vernon Police Department] located a door to the basement that was blocked by some kind of cabinet." Patrolman Arnold moved the obstruction from the door, and Glazier was the first one to go down the stairs into the basement. At the bottom of the basement stairs there was a doorway to the right; Glazier looked that way and suddenly observed a person lying on a sleeping bag on top of a pile of leaves. He pointed his weapon and flashlight at the person and yelled at them to show their hands. A young female sat up, and Glazier saw that she was bound in various places with duct tape and her hands and feet were bound with yellow rope. She sat up and looked directly at Glazier.

The female that Glazier had just yelled at was thirteen-year-old kidnap victim Sarah Maynard.

SEVENTEEN

The Girl on the Bed of Leaves

After what seemed an eternity of being locked in almost total darkness, Sarah Maynard realized she was being rescued. It was a moment she would never forget. She recalled later, "I heard someone come into the house, and they yelled, 'Get down, get down!' Then they came downstairs, and I think they kept saying, 'I think she's here!' And then a whole bunch of guys came down, and at first I thought they were bad guys. But then I saw the helmets on them, and I knew they were saving me!"

When the shock of seeing Sarah bound and lying on a bed of leaves wore off, both Sergeant Troy Glazier and Detective Craig Feeney proceeded to assist her. Glazier recalled, "Once it was apparent she was not in any immediate danger, I slowed everything down and had an officer go upstairs to get a camera before we released her from her bonds. A minute later Feeney took photos of Sarah and how she was bound before we released her. Other officers cleared the rest of the basement and I moved two large black trash bags that felt like they had leaves in them from the doorway to the right of where the female was."

Glazier debated getting onto a ledge that seemed to lead to a crawl space but decided against it because "there were some scuff marks in the fine dirt that appeared to have been made by a shoe." In other words he did not want to disturb the shoe prints in case they were important.

"Feeney and I released the female from the rope that she was bound with," Glazier recounted. "I untied the knots of the yellow rope that held her hands. Feeney cut the rope to her ankles to preserve the knots. Once she was free, we helped her stand up. She had [on] a white plastic bag that had holes cut out for her legs, so that she was wearing like a makeshift diaper. It appeared that she had urinated in her jeans because they were wet from her waist to halfway down to her knees."

For his part, Feeney remembered, "The girl had brown jersey gloves on her hands and they were duct-taped. Her hands were tied up with yellow rope and so were her ankles. I identified who we were and asked if she was okay. The girl advised that she was okay."

Sarah's first words to the officers took them completely by surprise. She said, "I have to get to school."

Despite everything that had happened, Sarah was afraid that she would be in trouble for missing so many days of school.

Detective Feeney assured her that she didn't need to go to school right away. Then, he reported, "after the photographs were taken, the girl asked if the suspect was secured so he couldn't hurt her. They assured her that he was. Then she said, 'He cut my finger with a knife, usually had me gagged, and he was going to release me before Christmas.'"

Feeney asked her if she knew where anyone else was— meaning Tina, Kody or Stephanie—and Sarah said that she didn't know, but she thought that the man who had held her captive had killed her dog.

Feeney helped Sarah get up, and she was of course still disoriented from having been in the dark for so long. Sergeant Glazier recalled, "We told her again that she was safe and that the Sheriff's Office was handling the investigation and they would be speaking with her shortly about what happened. We asked her if there had been anyone else at the residence besides her and the suspect that she knew about. She said no, and believed it had just been the two of them there." Although she was not as certain if her captor had someone outside the house helping him.

Glazier continued, "The suspect was taken from the residence area and secured in a KCSO cruiser. We called for a medic unit to respond to check on Sarah and transport her to Knox County Hospital (KCH). We helped her upstairs and stayed with her in the living room until the medics came in with a stretcher. Sarah was briefly checked by the medics and placed on the stretcher and covered with a blanket. She was taken out and transported to KCH for treatment and evaluation. The suspect was transported to KCSO."

Special Agent Joe Dietz arrived at Matthew Hoffman's house just as Sarah was being led up the stairs from the basement. Dietz accompanied her to Knox County Hospital; as they rode together to the hospital in the back of the ambulance, he monitored her treatment and asked her some questions about her abduction and captivity.

Sarah remembered later how strange it felt to her to actually be speaking to someone other than the man who had abducted her. She said, "I was glad they were helping me, but it was kind of freaky talking to anyone at the time." As yet she didn't even know Hoffman's name. She was sure she had never seen him before and couldn't imagine why her family had been targeted. She was also having a hard time adjusting to all the light. She had been in almost total darkness for so long that daylight seemed dazzling to her eyes.

Sarah told Dietz that she and her brother had been attacked after entering their home on Wednesday when they got home from school. "I told the investigators that me and Kody saw the blood on the tile and there was nobody in there. We were like, 'Oh my gosh'—and then he came and snatched us." Sarah told Dietz that the man had tried to grab her, but she broke free and ran to her bedroom. She hadn't actually seen him kill Kody, but she was worried that Kody had not survived.

Sarah said that the man came to her bedroom, grabbed her and carried her down to the basement where he used some available rope to tie her up. He then took her to the kitchen floor and left her there for a long time before taking her to Stephanie Sprang's Jeep and placing her inside of it.

After a while, Sarah told them, he drove her to the Pipesville Road ball field parking lot, which she recognized, and she was left in the backseat of the Jeep, covered with blankets, for another long period of time. Later, the man came back, placed her in a different car and drove her to the house where she was later found.

Sarah told Dietz that she had been tied up most of the time and had spent some time in a bathroom and some in a closet before being transferred to the small dark area in the basement. She was vague about when these movements occurred because her sense of time had been eroded by this point. Sarah did say that the man would not tell her what had happened to her mother, brother or Stephanie, but she suspected that he had killed all of them.

In the hospital, BCI&I Special Agent Mark Kollar photographed the work gloves and duct tape that Hoffman had used on Sarah. Then Kollar took possession of several pieces of evidence, including a binding from Sarah's right wrist, a binding from her left wrist, a bag containing socks and boots, another bag containing her clothing, and a kit connected to sexual molestation collected during the nurse's examination of Sarah.

Special Agent Dietz stayed with Sarah until Carrie
Huffman, a caseworker from Ohio's Child and Family Services, and Tom Bumpus, the KCSO detective in
charge of crimes against children, arrived, followed
shortly by Diana Oswalt, the victim advocate from the
Knox County Prosecutor's Office.

Diana Oswalt had been with many victims in Knox
County, but had never been involved with anything like
this. She'd come into her job by an unusual route; although she had always wanted to help people in need.
Until the late 1990s, Oswalt had worked at banks in
various capacities. She'd moved from one position to another, then finally told her husband it was time for a new
start. He agreed with her, and Oswalt put in an application to become a victim's advocate in Knox County.

Oswalt's immediate concern for Sarah was to assure
her that she was now safe and that the suspect could no
longer hurt her. He was in jail and would not be getting
back out. Sarah had some concerns that Matthew Hoffman had an accomplice, and Oswalt assured Sarah that
even if that was true, she would be well protected now
and nobody could hurt her.

Messages were flying all over the place by early Sunday
afternoon. Greg Borders was contacted about Sarah's
safe recovery by KCSO. He phoned Captain Shaffer
wanting to know if he should go to the hospital. Sarah
was told by authorities that her uncles, Tina's brothers,
had arrived at the hospital and wanted to see her, but

Sarah kept saying that she wanted her father, Larry Maynard. The only person she asked to see was her dad.

Larry and his family were stunned when they got the news that Sarah was alive. His first thoughts were filled with elation. "My daughter is alive!" And then the implication of what he'd just heard hit him hard; nothing had been said about Kody, Tina or Stephanie. What had happened to them? Were they alive as well?

Larry hurried to the hospital. He recalled, "It was all surreal going into the place. I don't even know what I was thinking by that point. I was beyond thinking. I went into a room, and there she was. We just both went over and hugged each other. We didn't say a word. Just hugged each other as tightly as we could. I was crying like a baby. This went on for ten or fifteen minutes before we said anything."

All day long there had been a mob of reporters swirling around the Maynard residence, KCSO headquarters, Matthew Hoffman's residence. Diana Oswalt did her best to help the Maynard family cope with the reporters and to shield them from the media onslaught coming in from all sides, though in many ways, it was just as new to her as it was to the Maynards. Nothing of this magnitude had ever befallen any of them before.

Later that Sunday, Sheriff David Barber held a press conference. He announced, "We have good news to report today. We have located and rescued Sarah Maynard at approximately 8:00 AM this morning. She was being held against her will, and she was in good condition with non-life-threatening injuries. She was taken to the hospital for evaluation. She has been interviewed somewhat. In the house with her was an individual from Mount Vernon. He is now in the Knox County Jail currently charged with kidnapping. His name is Matthew J. Hoffman, and he is thirty years old. We believe Sarah was under the control of Mr. Hoffman since last Wednesday in one form or another and at one location or another."

There were of course a lot of questions about Matthew Hoffman from reporters. To these, Sheriff Barber replied, "We are unsure at this time if Hoffman was acquainted with the family. That remains to be seen as the investigation continues. Mr. Hoffman does have a prior conviction in Colorado, for which he served prison time. Mr. Hoffman's residence on Columbus Road is currently being processed by the Bureau of Criminal Identification and Investigation. It is being considered a crime scene and treated as such."

To a question about whether Tina, Kody and Stephanie were dead, Barber answered, "As of right now, we have no one we are aware of who is deceased. Tomorrow, we hope DNA testing can begin. We have been assured this will be considered a priority case by the BCI&I."

After Matt Hoffman was arrested and Sarah Maynard was freed from her basement captivity, BCI&I agents began the long process of collecting, photographing and cataloguing the evidence at Matthew Hoffman's home.

BCI&I Special Agent Gary Wilgus wrote later, "The residence was photographed as it was found, room by room, starting on the ground floor. I then photographed the basement area as it was found. At the bottom of the stairway just to the left was a hole cut through the block wall leading into a dark room where blankets and bedding had been placed on the leaf covered floor."

BCI&I Agent George Staley Jr. was also at Hoffman's house and photographed the whole residence, room by room, placing numbered placards at each key area. Item number 1 was a pair of Starter brand athletic shoes that had characteristics similar to the footwear impressions found in Tina Herrmann's house. Item 2 was a pair of boots that matched some of the other impressions found at the house.

Item 3 was a camouflaged T-shirt identical to the one the individual caught on the security camera tape had been wearing at Walmart around midnight on November 10. The next item of significance, item 5, was a Canon PowerShot A470 camera found in a dresser drawer on the ground floor. The camera was later accessed and photographs of Sarah Maynard were identified on the camera. These were photos of Sarah during her ordeal at Hoffman's house.

Another item of importance, number 5.2, was a leather sap or blackjack found in the same dresser, and item 6 was a large SOG brand sheath-type knife, also found in the dresser drawer. Item 9 was a piece of rope found in the basement at the bottom of the stairway. Law enforcement officers later informed Staley that this piece of rope had been used to bind Sarah and had been cut by them to preserve the original knots. Other items included a roll of gray duct tape, and a blue blanket that had been used to cover Sarah. Also in the basement area were a sweatshirt, two more blankets, a pillow and more gray duct tape.

Three computers were found in various parts of the house, as well as one thousand dollars in cash stuffed inside an envelope. An LG brand flip phone was collected from the ground floor, a Casio flip phone from one kitchen drawer and a Motorola flip phone from another.

Though two of the most interesting items discovered in the residence were a bone and an apparent bloodstain, later testing would prove that neither came from a human.

EIGHTEEN

"I Knew I Had Done Something Wrong"

The *Mount Vernon News* was one of the first print news organizations to report Sarah's recovery. The headline stated, "One found; man in custody; search continues."

Reporters started scrambling in every direction, talking to Matt Hoffman's neighbors on Columbus Road, digging into his past, going out to where Larry Maynard lived in Franklin County.

Dawna Davis, Hoffmann's next-door neighbor, told reporters she started keeping her children away from Hoffman because he was so weird. She said, "The only interaction I had with him was over his dog. I talked to the man through a window about his dog attacking our dog in our yard." She went on to describe the way Hoffman had interacted with her children, and his actions against his girlfriend before she'd left him.

THE GIRL IN THE LEAVES

As for the Sunday morning SWAT raid at Hoffmann's home, Davis said, "I had just gotten up and was on the computer talking to my aunt, and heard a great big boom. I opened my window and saw all those officers with their guns drawn. I didn't know what was going on!"

Dawna and her three children had to stay in their house, by orders of the police, until 2:00 PM Sunday. As soon as she was given the all-clear from the police, Dawna grabbed her kids and dog and left the house in a hurry.

In a more detailed news conference, Sheriff David Barber related to reporters how the SWAT raid had rescued Sarah Maynard and was the result of investigative efforts by sheriff's office detectives and others. Barber said, "Unfortunately, as of this time, we have not located Tina, Stephanie or Kody. Hoffman has not given us any information and has not been cooperative at this point. The residence on Columbus Road is currently being processed by the Bureau of Criminal Identification and Investigation. It's being considered a crime scene and treated as such."

Sheriff Barber went on to say that "a significant amount of blood" had been found in Tina Herrmann's residence on King Beach Drive. He added that police had searched sections of Apple Valley Lake and Foundation Park, where a wooded area was now taped off. This probably came about because some of Matt Hoffman's neighbors told FBI agents that Hoffman often took walks through there. There was a section where a former gravel pit had been turned into a recreation area with small ponds. Authorities were concerned about what those ponds might hold.

Barber related that aircraft from the Ohio State Highway Patrol were flying over locations in the county, using infrared scanners. Other officers were on quad runners, going over the rural areas of the county.

Before the news of Sarah's rescue had begun to spread, friends, family and concerned citizens of Apple Valley had gathered at the Apple Valley Property Owner's Association office on Sunday, November 14, 2010, to start a new day of searching. Stephen Thompson, Stephanie's father, thanked all of the volunteers for their time, and then volunteers Jennifer and Brian Kessler, who were coordinating volunteer efforts, organized the people into groups and gave them directions as to where to begin their searches. Around three hundred people showed up that day.

The Kesslers also gave out these instructions: "We ask that if you find something, to back away, mark where you saw it and immediately call the sheriff's office. We don't want to ruin anything, so please be careful. If there are any locations you think we should check out, please let us know."

The volunteers headed out in teams. One team of nine, headed by Brian Kessler, went down Magers Road to a location along Little Jelloway Creek, while another team that included Robin Scoles, who was just one of many volunteers, searched around Bennett Park and Skyline Drive. Robin told a reporter, "If it was me or my daughter missing, I would want people to look for us."

And then volunteers' cell phones started ringing with the news that Sarah Maynard had been found alive. It brought both hope and fear about the fate of the others. If one had been found alive, maybe the others would be too—but if so, why hadn't they been with Sarah, and why was there so much blood in Tina Herrmann's home?

While some decided to give up searching once Sarah had been found, others poured in to start new search groups. In one of these was Elizabeth Foor, who described herself as a concerned parent. She said, "I have two daughters, and it's so sad to hear this has happened. I knew I had to come out to help."

One search party found two shirts along a gravel road on the east side of Apple Valley. The shirts looked as if they had been ripped and were draped over a tree limb. Felicia White, a friend of Stephanie Sprang's, phoned KCSO to inform them of what they had just found. She thought one of the shirts might have been something Stephanie had worn. Awhile later, a KCSO deputy arrived, took the shirt and thanked the volunteers for their efforts.

Felicia later told a reporter, "I'm so thankful for all the prayers and community support. When I heard about what happened, I knew I couldn't let it go. I had to help. I just want everyone to know that [Stephanie's] a great person and a great mom. She would never leave her kids for any reason. I'm not going to give up. Never going to give up until they're found."

Because of the discovery of Sarah alive, the complaint against Matthew Hoffman was enlarged by Detective David Light. He noted in the formal complaint that "on or about the 11th day of November 2010, Matthew J. Hoffman did commit kidnapping, by force, threat or deception. He did remove Sarah Maynard from the place where she was found, with the purpose to facilitate the commission of a felony of flight thereafter, a felony of the first degree."

With Sarah safe, the KCSO officers had much to do at the house on Columbus Road. Sergeant Troy Glazier recalled, "Once the scene was secure, Deputy Minot started a crime scene log. This was shortly turned over to [Detective Craig] Feeney, who logged everyone entering the scene. A convoy of BCI&I and FBI vehicles came to the location once it was secured to begin processing evidence. [Detective] Feeney and I briefly spoke with an FBI Agent and advised him of our entry and some things we observed inside the residence as well as our contact with Sarah.

Captain Shaffer requested that we leave two ESU Team members at the scene to assist them. [Detective] Feeney stayed to continue the crime scene log, and Patrolman [Tim] Arnold also stayed to assist with anything else that was needed. The rest of the MVPD ESU team loaded up and went to the police department for a short debriefing." To say they had had an eventful morning was to compare a hill to Mount Everest.

Matthew Hoffman had, of course, been booked at the KCSO headquarters. It was noted that he was Caucasian, stood six feet, one inch tall, and weighed 185 pounds. His hair and eyes were brown. He had recently turned thirty; his date of birth was noted as November 1, 1980.

Hoffman's clothing was taken from him and stored as evidence. Items included a pair of black sweatpants, a white T-shirt, a red sweatshirt, one pair of white socks and a blue and yellow hat. He also had to submit to two buccal DNA swabs and two penis swabs.

Concurrent to all the dramatic events happening on Columbus Road, FBI Special Agent Harry Trombitas and KCSO Lieutenant Gary Rohler had been in Apple Valley, talking with Matthew Hoffman's mother and stepfather. As they were speaking with the parents, Rohler was suddenly informed that the suspect was in custody, and was requested to come in to help interview Hoffman.

As soon as Lieutenant Rohler arrived at KCSO headquarters, he met with Detective Sergeant Roger Brown and the two men went in to interview Hoffman. Hoffman was read his rights and shown the KCSO statement of rights form. He waived his right to a lawyer, but from the very beginning Hoffman refused to answer any questions put to him by either Rohler or Brown. He pantomimed that his heart was broken, but did not utter a word during questioning, which lasted for hours. Of course, the main questions were, "Where are Tina, Kody and Stephanie, and are they still alive?" But Hoffman gave no clue as to what their fates might have been.

Detective Sergeant Brown noted during this time, "For over the next three hours we attempted to get Matthew to speak to us, but he would not respond. On occasion he would nod his head and drink his water, but continued not to speak. He would close his eyes for long periods of time, put his head down on the desk and occasionally shed tears." The videotaped session also revealed that at times, Hoffman would yawn.

The interrogation went on and on despite Hoffman's irresponsiveness. Finally BCI&I Special Agent Joe Dietz entered the room and after about fifteen minutes, was able to convince Hoffman to speak the first words he'd said to anyone for several hours. Hoffman said that he was having a hard time figuring out what had happened. Then, after a long pause, he claimed that he'd "found" Sarah in his house, so he figured that he must have done something wrong.

Hoffman continued with this bizarre version of events: "I found her in the house and she was tied up. So I took care of her. I found her on Thursday and I didn't know how she had gotten there, but she told me I had 'done it.' I knew I had done something wrong, but I didn't know what it was and I was trying to piece things together."

Hoffman added that he didn't know Sarah prior to

coming across her tied up in his basement. After making these few statements, Hoffman once again became unresponsive to all questioning. Since they were getting nowhere, the officers concluded the interview a short time later on Sunday evening.

NINETEEN

A Flood of Tips

Authorities continued their work at Hoffman's house, photographing, collecting and cataloguing a variety of items. In addition to the strange drawings on the bathroom wall that Sarah had noticed, the most unusual were the many bags of leaves, which were attached to the walls and scattered around the house. Every square inch of open space along the walls was taken up with these bags. There were also loose leaves scattered around the floor, and bags that had not yet been filled. It was as if the purpose of the whole house was to become a repository for leaves. None of the leaves had been there when Hoffman's girlfriend moved out only weeks previously.

Items were being seized from Matt Hoffman's silver Toyota Yaris as well. These included a used roll of duct tape, a Lowe's store receipt in a trash bag and a receipt from a Mount Vernon Duchess Shoppe (a gas station convenience store). There was a receipt from McDonald's, a sandwich container on the backseat and a Walmart bag. Also seized was a small suitcase with tree-climbing gear inside. One of the more ominous findings was a folding saw in a suitcase on the front passenger seat.

Every bit of evidence was looked at, no matter how small. Anything could hold a clue as to where Tina, Kody and Stephanie were. The items were like scattered pieces of a jigsaw puzzle, and the investigators still had no idea what the total puzzle looked like.

On November 14, a strange call came in to KCSO at 7:36 PM. A message sheet was notated, "Detectives, Captain or Whoever—Ron Metcalf is demanding to speak with someone about yesterday and wants a protection order." Just what the protection order was all about was not mentioned on the form.

Around the same time, a Kelly G left a message for Captain Shaffer: "There is a smell outside the humane society. It smells like something decaying." And a woman who would not give her name told detectives to check the Caves Campground.

A man named Mike M reported, "I was friends with Matt Hoffman before he went to Colorado. Matthew is very familiar with the Apple Valley clubhouse area and also the spillway area." Then Mike said that Hoffman had been hanging around with a certain male friend since getting back from Colorado, and Mike gave that person's name.

Matt Cox, principal of Mount Vernon Middle School,

related that a student told him that he used to go swimming with Matthew Hoffman and "do other things" with him. KCSO later contacted this student.

Larry H told the dispatcher at KCSO, "Friday evening, by Riverside Park, there was a guy, tall and thin, looking over the bridge. He had a kid with him who looked to be about six to ten years old."

And Carolyn H noted that on Thursday night after dark, at 7:00 PM, she heard a vehicle stop by a tan house to the right of hers, directly behind which were some woods. She heard someone get out of the vehicle. The person was nearby, and she could hear a lot of rustling of leaves. It scared her so badly she ran back into her house.

People also called to share specific details about Matthew Hoffman. A man told KCSO, "Matthew Hoffman likes to cut through Foundation Park with his car. He almost hit me there one day."

Kathy M said, "Heard a long thud and loud scream at about 3:30 AM in the morning earlier in the week." This was in an area near Hoffman's residence.

An individual named Mike B related that on Wednesday, November 10, between 3:00 and 4:00 PM, he was on the Kokosing Gap Trail heading west just past the railroad bridge and there were two people below the bridge. Mike said, "There was a girl sitting on her butt with her hands behind her. A man was kneeling in front of her. The female had some clothes laying in front of her."

Mark M contacted authorities and said, "Across the street from a rental equipment company is a white barn. Behind that are four-wheel trails. Matthew and I used to go back there and hang out. We were back there all the time."

Another person got in contact with an officer and related, "Check trees for evidence. Matt talked about living in trees. He always carried ropes and a chain saw in his trunk."

Some of the tips were coming in from much farther afield than the local community. Ron F of Chicago claimed to have spotted the two missing women and boy in Chicago. Stanley O of Chattanooga, Tennessee, was sure he'd spotted the women and boy at a Raceway Gas Station there.

Another strange tip came in from a woman named Cornella K from Rhode Island. She stated from the photograph she saw, Matthew Hoffman appeared to have "a very peculiar messed-up nose and twisted ears. Genetic abnormalities which affect the physical body to such an extent tend to also affect the brain and glands." Cornella thought that Hoffman's lawyer should become involved so that he could find an expert analyst in such abnormalities. This expert might persuade Hoffman to reveal where the missing three people were. Cornella signed off, "Doing all in the name/reputation of the Lord Jesus the Christ."

Gary C of Long Beach, California, claimed, "I'm a psychic from California. Kokosing Gap Trail at the intersection of State Route 36 goes under State Route 36 southwest and northeast. Take the trail south for one thousand feet. Another small trail runs along that trail. Go east to Howard Street in Howard. Where two trails

branch off is where bodies are covered with red plastic."
A later note by authorities related that the Knox County
Emergency Management Agency director Brian Hess
went there, but found nothing.

Another psychic phoned in and said, "The three others are still alive. They are being held by a white male
forty-five to fifty-five years old. He is of medium build
and rough looking. He is unemployed and staying in a
house owned by his mother. This is in an adjacent county,
probably east of Mount Vernon. He knows the family or
a family friend, and has done work around the house. He
used a weapon to get them in an older van or SUV. The
suspect in jail knows this subject and will crack during
interrogation."

KCSO by Sunday evening was nearly overwhelmed by the
amount of work they were now tasked with. Assignments
included the ongoing search of Matthew Hoffman's residence and seizure of items therein; the interrogation of
Hoffman, who had yet to divulge what had happened to
Tina, Kody and Stephanie; the taking in and logging of
the tips; the coordination of volunteer search efforts; and
the dispensing of news to the hoard of television and
print journalists whose news vehicles and satellite trucks
were camped out in the KCSO parking lot. This last matter was a huge headache for the office in general and for
Sheriff David Barber in particular. Nothing like this had
ever happened in Knox County before.

To help in this regard, FBI Special Agent Harry Trom-

In 1997, Tina Herrmann and Larry Maynard had a baby daughter, Sarah.
(LARRY MAYNARD)

Not long after, Sarah's baby brother, Kody, was born, and she doted on him.
(LARRY MAYNARD)

Sarah was proud of her little brother, who excelled in academics and sports.
(LARRY MAYNARD)

By 2010, Tina Herrmann (pictured) and her kids lived in the quiet neighborhood of Apple Valley near beautiful Apple Valley Lake. (LARRY MAYNARD)

Stephanie Sprang was a neighbor of Tina Herrmann and one of her best friends. She too went missing on November 10, 2010. (OHIO DMV)

Investigators discovered large bloodstains in Tina Herrmann's home, making them worry about the fate of the missing individuals.
(KNOX COUNTY SHERIFF'S OFFICE)

Knox County Sheriff David Barber and his team of investigators worked tirelessly on the case.
(ROBERT SCOTT)

Hundreds of citizen volunteers signed up to help search for Stephanie, Tina, Kody and Sarah. They also held prayer vigils at this town square in Mount Vernon, Ohio.
(ROBERT SCOTT)

Matthew Hoffman of Mount Vernon, Ohio, had been in trouble with the law, even as a young man. (KNOX COUNTY SHERIFF'S OFFICE)

When Hoffman was nineteen years old, he stole this large sign in Steamboat Springs, Colorado, and also burned down a condominium complex there. (ROBERT SCOTT)

Investigators were able to track Hoffman down as the suspect in the missing persons' case concerning Tina, Sarah, Kody and Stephanie. (KNOX COUNTY DISTRICT ATTORNEY'S OFFICE)

On the morning of November 14, 2010, a SWAT team burst into Matthew Hoffman's house and arrested him there. (ROBERT SCOTT)

The officers found Sarah Maynard alive and tied up on a bed of leaves in Hoffman's basement. (KNOX COUNTY SHERIFF'S OFFICE)

Hoffman had also covered his floors with dried leaves and had bags of leaves stacked up in every room. (KNOX COUNTY SHERIFF'S OFFICE)

Investigators also found strange images drawn in Hoffman's bathroom, where he had kept Sarah tied up part of the time.
(KNOX COUNTY SHERIFF'S OFFICE)

In exchange for having the death penalty removed, Matthew Hoffman revealed where he had hidden the dismembered bodies of Tina, Kody and Stephanie. (KNOX COUNTY SHERIFF'S OFFICE)

He had placed them in a hollow tree in a nature preserve. A tree cutter had to cut a hole in the tree to remove trash bags filled with body parts. (KNOX COUNTY SHERIFF'S OFFICE)

Larry and Sarah Maynard created a foundation to help other victims of crime—the Tina Rose B. Herrmann and Kody Alexander Maynard Healing Hearts Memorial Fund.
(LARRY MAYNARD)

Tina Rose B. Herrmann
1978 – 2010

Kody Alexander Maynard
1999 – 2010

A memorial had grown over time at Tina's house where the crimes had been committed. Even a year later, people still placed flowers and mementos there.
(ROBERT SCOTT)

Larry and Sarah attended the foundation's first annual hot air balloon festival, which raised money for the Healing Hearts fund.
(LARRY MAYNARD)

bitas made a list of suggestions about how to deal with the media and what information to dispense to them. Sheriff Barber was grateful for the advice and used it as a template in his remarks to reporters.

Trombitas started out by suggesting that the sheriff release this statement: "Based on evidence discovered at the two crime scenes and what investigators have learned through various interviews, the Knox County Sheriff's Office is moving into a new phase of the investigation, and we are now conducting a two-pronged investigative approach.

"Prong one deals with the blood at the initial scene and the recovery of Sarah. Investigators are considering the possibility that the three missing persons may have in fact been killed." Trombitas added that because of what was known so far, the bodies of the three may have been moved to an undisclosed location by Matt Hoffman or someone helping him, and suggested that KCSO now ask all citizens of the region to think back to the afternoon of Wednesday, November 10, or Thursday, November 11, and report any unusual sightings of suspicious persons or activity they may have witnessed. Citizens of the county, especially in rural areas near Mount Vernon and Apple Valley, should search their properties for recent tire marks or places where a person could have driven in with a vehicle, especially in areas where there was concealing foliage or outbuildings. The statement also instructed people not touch anything that looked suspicious, but to call KCSO immediately.

Prong two dealt with the chance that Tina, Kody and

Stephanie could still be alive. Trombitas told Barber, "Now may be a good time to give the media photos of the three known vehicles involved—the Toyota Yaris, the pickup and Jeep. Sometimes seeing an image is far superior in jogging the memory of a citizen than just a verbal description."

Trombitas ended his message to Sheriff Barber by stating he would advise not giving out any additional information about the two crime scenes—Tina's home on King Beach Drive and Matt Hoffman's residence on Columbus Road—and he also suggested that Sheriff Barber schedule formal press conferences at specific hours each day.

Larry Maynard and his family had their own challenges dealing with the swarm of media that surrounded their home. Never in their wildest dreams had any of them ever imagined they would be placed in such a position.

Larry recalled, "There were news vans and satellite trucks all up and down [our] street. The reporters were constantly ringing the door bell, and at first I just told them I wasn't giving any interviews. After a while I put up a sign, 'Don't ring the doorbell or knock. Please respect our privacy.' It didn't help. They kept ringing the door bell and asking for interviews anyway.

"Phone calls were coming in from everywhere. Local news stations and national ones. We were even getting calls from overseas. And talk shows were calling as well.

The phone wouldn't stop ringing. We felt like we were trapped in our own house. It was horrible!

"We were hunkered down like prisoners in our own house. We had Sarah back, (she was at home with Larry and his family at that point) and that was great. But we couldn't stop worrying about Kody, Tina and Stephanie. I could barely eat. I could barely sleep. I'd just go from a daze into kind of half-sleep. Even then, it was mostly just falling into a daze in a chair."

At 7:15 PM on November 14, an interesting development took place. BCI&I Special Agent Joe Dietz convinced Matthew Hoffman to take a ride with him in an effort to refresh his memory about what had occurred. As Dietz wrote in a report, "Detective [Doug] Turpen, Special Agent [Kristin] Cadieux and I accompanied Hoffman on this drive to different parts of Knox County."

The investigators' reports later stated precisely when and where they had gone, noting that they left the sheriff's office, drove to Hoffman's mother's house and then by Tina Herrmann's house. They went down Magers Road, turned around and went by Tina's house and again by Hoffman's mother's house once more. Then they drove to the ball fields at East Knox Middle School and later by the baseball field in Howard. They stopped off at a Burger King for some food, went on to Foundation Park and finally back to the sheriff's office.

Alas, the trip was a bust, as Hoffman did not reveal

anything as to where Tina, Kody and Stephanie might be found. Attempts to have Matthew Hoffman answer questions continued into Monday, November 15. Detective David Light noted, "He would occasionally drink some water, but would not even answer if he wanted a bathroom break. The efforts to have him speak included FBI Agent Kristin Cadieux, but he would not talk much about the incidents that led to his arrest."

Though investigators were determined to get information out of Matthew Hoffman, and they tried all the interrogation techniques standard in these kinds of interviews, Hoffman remained absolutely silent.

TWENTY

"The Epitome of Bravery"

Requests for interviews with Larry and Sarah Maynard only increased on Monday, November 15, 2010. Not only were radio outlets and newspaper journalists trying to talk to them, but representatives from *Good Morning America*, *Oprah*, *Maury* and many more national television programs were also calling. Even networks from overseas were interested in the story.

Larry said, "I didn't want to talk to any of them. We just had gotten Sarah back, and our main concerns were about what had happened to Tina, Kody and Stephanie. I just wanted the world to go away and leave me alone. But the phone kept ringing, and the media was camped all around us."

* * *

Sheriff David Barber gave his afternoon press conference on November 15, following FBI Special Agent Harry Trombitas's suggestions, and revealed a few more facts about the ongoing investigation. Barber said, "We're here to give you an update on the investigation. The positive aspect of the investigation occurred yesterday morning at approximately 8:00 AM with the rescue of thirteen-year-old Sarah Maynard. Sarah is with family members now. She was examined at a local hospital and treated at a local hospital. She has been reunited with family members and is doing well.

"As a result of the investigation and as a result of Sarah's rescue and the arrest of Matthew Hoffman, our investigation has taken a turn in a little bit different direction. It kind of has a two-pronged approach now. Obviously with her rescue we still want to remain optimistic that Tina, Stephanie and Kody are alive and being held against their will at some location. That makes it important for the public to think back to what they were doing last Wednesday or Thursday. Did they see something unusual? Something before all this became an event. Did they see someone unusual in the area? A car parked somewhere or something like that. If so, I would like them to please, please, please call the sheriff's office. We do have a tip line in place. We need that kind of information—whether it's vehicles or something that didn't seem quite right.

"The other approach to the investigation is, unfortunately when you have a situation like this, when you've had four missing people for almost a week and there's

been no contact with them with the exception of Sarah—
we have to approach this investigation that Tina, Stephanie and Kody are dead. That they have been killed.

"That makes it crucial that if a person sees something—something out of the ordinary, don't touch it.
Don't assume it belongs there. It could be clothing, a
bag, something like that, it could contain evidence with
which we need to further the investigation.

"We are continuing with search efforts, and I think a
lot of you [the media] have seen that this morning. That's
where we are today. I will take questions now. I will re-
mind you, this is an active investigation. There is a lot of
sensitive information that could impede a successful prosecution, so there are some questions I will not be able to
answer."

The first questions asked were about recent police
searches in Foundation Park and whether there had been
anything specific in the park that led them there.

Barber said no, and explained, "Most of you know
that Matthew Hoffman lives at Columbus Road. Right
across the street is a lane that leads into that park. Foundation Park has ponds and it's a former gravel pit. That's
why we're searching."

In fact, down in Foundation Park, the Ohio Department of Natural Resources had conducted a search of the
water areas via a boat equipped with sonar. They located
two objects in the water and called in dive team members
from the Fredericktown Fire Department. The objects
were discovered to be two vehicles submerged in the
water. This caused a lot of excitement, but ultimately nei-

ther turned out to have any connection to the case. One was an older model Mercury Grand Marquis full of dirt and sediment that had clearly been in the water for quite a while. The other was a Ford Expedition that investigators learned had been stolen in 2006.

When asked whether Matthew Hoffman had been cooperative in the investigation, Barber was guarded. "I won't comment on what he has or has not been doing," he said, adding only, "The investigators are talking with him, and I think most people when they're arrested— they're not too likely to want to talk about it. That's all I want to say."

Questions turned to the three people still missing.

"Have you found out if there was a connection between Mr. Hoffman and these four people?" a journalist inquired.

Barber answered, "Other than that he has a relative who lives within walking distance, not at this time."

"You said that Sarah had been in his possession, whatever you want to call it, of Mr. Hoffman dating back to Wednesday. What is the last time Sarah saw those other three individuals?"

Barber responded that Sarah had last seen her mother and brother on Wednesday, and he wasn't sure about Stephanie, though it had possibly been on the Tuesday.

One reporter asked, "You said that you're hopeful that [the three missing people are] alive, but there is the possibility that they're dead. Which way are you leaning on that?"

Barber answered, "I have to be realistic. It's been all this time and evidence that's been gathered, and evidence discovered yesterday—well, with the families, we're making sure they're aware of the ultimate possibility in this."

"When did you start to believe that Tina, Stephanie and Kody might be dead?" a journalist asked.

Barber said, "We still are hopeful that they are alive. But we have to be realistic that the amount of blood in the house and the fact that Sarah was found with the suspect and no one else was found there, and no one has seen them since Wednesday of last week—that is troubling."

This was followed by, "Were all four people alive when they left the house?" Barber said he didn't know the answer to that.

"With these lives in the balance, how far can you push Matthew Hoffman for answers?" Barber was asked.

"Everything within the law," he replied.

Someone asked, "Is the search confined only locally? Or is there a plan to expand it out of state?"

Barber replied, "At this time there's no reason to believe the three missing persons are outside the geographical area of Knox County."

"Can you address how you and your officers are handling all of this?"

For a moment Sheriff Barber was facetious and said, "We just don't sleep." Then he added, "But in all seriousness, because of the partnership we have with the FBI, with the attorney general's office, BCI&I, Franklin County Sheriff's Office, Delaware County Sheriff's Office and other agencies, we work around the clock, rotating people in and rotating people out."

A reporter wondered if the sheriff's office had a person of interest other than Matthew Hoffman in mind. Barber answered, "Not at this time. There's nothing to indicate that he had an accomplice. But the investigation is still in progress."

"Can you comment on Sarah's health condition right now?"

"It's my understanding that physically she's fine. Obviously she's been through a lot and she's going to be recovering from that with the help of services."

"Have you gotten any information from her?"

"Investigators have."

"Have her statements been helpful?"

"Absolutely."

"Have the suspect's parents, who live near the home— have they been cooperative?"

"They have been cooperative."

Another reporter asked if Barber could go into more detail about Sarah. Barber stated, "She is a very brave little girl. I have not met her in person yet. My investigators have talked to her, and I'm looking forward to the day I get to meet Sarah Maynard, because not only is she assisting the investigation, but under the circumstances, a thirteen-year-old girl being held captive for days by a stranger—I would call that the epitome of bravery."

A reporter asked how long Sarah had been bound and gagged during her captivity. Barber said, "I'm not going to be specific, but I think she told us she had not been bound and gagged the whole time."

"Did he hurt her or assault her in any way?"

Barber responded, "I can't comment on that."

A reporter asked what Sheriff Barber thought of all the citizen volunteers out searching. He said, "I think it's outstanding. But they need to be mindful that they're not used to doing these sorts of things. They need to be organized so that they're not contaminating evidence by just tromping around. If they see something out of the ordinary, they need to step back and let an officer know about it."

One reporter brought up the fact that some of Hoffman's neighbors said that he had been acting strangely in the days before all of this happened. Barber replied, "Those folks will be interviewed by law enforcement. And no matter how insignificant it may sound, anything like that, that people remember, they should call the sheriff's office. It's going to be followed up by law enforcement."

"Is Greg Borders, the ex-boyfriend, a person of interest?"

Sheriff Barber gave an emphatic, "No."

The sheriff's news conference provided Larry Maynard no new answers. He wanted to go out with one of the search parties, but family and friends were against this. They worried what would happen if he stumbled upon

Tina's and Kody's bodies. Although they still held out hope that Tina and Kody were alive, the prospects of that were dimming by the hour.

While the Maynards tried to cope, the tips continued to pour into KCSO.

Todd K said that he'd seen one of the missing women in a green minivan. And TJ, who stated that he worked for a cable company, said that while working close to Mathew Hoffman's house on Columbus Road on Friday, November 12, he'd seen a boxy black van parked in front of Hoffman's residence.

Doris D reported that over the weekend, two rough-looking men had come to her door asking about Stephanie. One of them had blue eyes and big arms and was very demanding.

Jeff S said he worked at the library at Kenyon College and he often walked on the paths near the Brown Family Environmental Center where Tina's pickup truck had been found. Jeff told an investigator that there were remains of a fire near a path. This was against the rules, and Jeff had learned that Matthew Hoffman had been convicted of arson. Jeff related, "Hoffman may have camped out on the path by the river."

Brenda R told an investigator that a pickup truck with a camper shell was parked about a quarter mile from Tina's residence. According to Brenda, the pickup had showed up two days before the people went missing. Someone told her that Hoffman drove a car, but recently he had been driving a pickup truck as well.

And Jay S said that on Friday morning, November 12,

"I saw a male matching Matthew's description, walking on Route 229 East toward Mount Vernon. He was just passing where the trail crosses 229 between Duff [Street] and Wiggins Street."

Monday evening, a private prayer vigil, closed to the media, was held at the South Vernon Methodist Church. Another, public prayer vigil, however, was held at the Public Square in Mount Vernon. Many people who did not personally know Sarah or the others who were still missing gathered there.

Megan Sowul of Mount Vernon was in that group and said, "We don't know them personally, but we know people who do know them. It's really sad. We have a nephew who is ten years old, and we can't imagine if this happened to him."

Jay Berger was there with his wife, Betty, and related, "We have children, and we certainly would want people praying for us. We came because we thought it was our duty, and who else can we turn to except our heavenly father?" The Bergers had driven to Mount Vernon from Mount Liberty, about ten miles away.

Pastor Dennis Eggerton led the crowd in prayer at the Public Square. His wife, Gennelle Eggerton, was the principal at the East Knox Elementary School and had known both Sarah and Kody personally. In part, Eggerton prayed, "Lord, it's times like these that people turn to you. Father, with our troubled hearts we come to you. Father, be with them. Give them strength. Keep us as a community ready to come alongside when the time is right, and teach us to bear the burden. We cry out to you at times like this when we have nowhere else to go. Be with the ones who need you the most."

Cameron Keller, who was in the crowd, told a journalist what many in the area felt: "We're all upset. We're just completely taken aback by what's happened in our small town. I just can't believe this could happen in Mount Vernon."

TWENTY-ONE

"I'm a Monster"

At 9:00 AM on November 16, 2010, in an interview room, BCI&I Special Agent Joe Dietz and FBI Special Agent Kristin Cadieux met once again at the Knox County Sheriff's Office. Just before Matthew Hoffman was brought into the interview room, he spoke privately with Dietz for a moment.

Dietz and Hoffman went into the interview room alone, while Agent Cadieux waited outside, and Hoffman told Dietz that he wanted all audio and video devices turned off. Then Hoffman asked Dietz to take him to the restroom. Agent Dietz agreed to do so, and remained in the restroom with Hoffman while Detective Doug Turpen was stationed right outside the door. Once Hoffman and Dietz were inside, Hoffman asked if there were any recording devices in the restroom or if Dietz had any on his person.

Upon Hoffman's request, Dietz went outside and handed his two cell phones to Detective Turpen and then returned to the restroom. Hoffman then told Dietz that during the night he had a dream about being at a food-processing plant. In the dream, Hoffman said, he opened up a trash bag and saw human body parts inside. He got a knot in his stomach, he said, and it started coming back to him.

Hoffman told Dietz that he now recalled some of what had happened, but that he wanted to reveal it in his own way. Hoffman said he wanted to write the location of the bodies down on a piece of paper and then have a legal document created through an attorney, who would hold on to the document until Hoffman was dead. Hoffman continued that he wanted Agent Dietz to arrange for Hoffman to take another drive outside the jail facility. Hoffman added, "I'll pretend to escape, and then I want you to shoot and kill me. After I'm dead, the attorney will reveal the location of the bodies."

Hoffman said he could not live with what he had done, and if this could not be agreed to, he planned to kill himself in jail anyway. He said he did not want to be injected with Thorazine for the rest of his life in prison. He'd rather die now. Hoffman seemed to believe that if he was sent to prison he would be given an antipsychotic drug for the rest of his life.

Agent Dietz said he couldn't agree to the drive or to shooting Hoffman, but that instead Hoffman should "re-lieve the pain in your gut by telling [us] where the bodies were hidden." Hoffman instead said that he would do so only if his plan were carried out. "I'm a monster and I can't live with what I've done! I just want to die! I saw horrible cut-up things," Hoffman said.

Dietz repeated that Hoffman would feel better if he just revealed where the bodies were, but instead Hoffman eventually claimed that he'd actually made up the story about remembering where the body parts were hidden, and added that he'd done that so he could get himself killed in the escape plan.

After this bizarre interlude in the restroom, Agent Dietz and Matt Hoffman returned to the interview room, where the official interview with both Agents Dietz and Cadieux continued, though with meager results.

Despite gleaning little useful information, investigators did note that Hoffman seemed more animated with a woman in the room than he had been with only the male detectives there. Detective David Light said later, "Special Agent Dietz and Special Agent Cadieux spoke to Hoffman again on Tuesday, November 16th. Hoffman advised them that he did not want an attorney and that it was in his best interest not to have one. The public defender's office was assigned to represent him for his bond hearing scheduled that day. Attorney Bruce Malek [of the Knox County Public Defenders Office] went to the sheriff's office and insisted on meeting with Hoffman immediately. Hoffman was asked again if he wished to see an attorney and he again said that he did not want an attorney.

"Officers continued to talk with Hoffman until advised by Knox County Prosecutor John Thatcher that they must stop the interview. Hoffman was then placed back in the jail, where an attorney made contact with him several hours before the bond hearing."

When it was time for the actual court hearing in Judge Paul Spurgeon's courtroom, Matthew Hoffman wasn't present. He was videoed from his jail cell, where he sat quietly next to Malek, rather than being escorted into the courtroom.

Hoffman was wearing a green padded "suicide gown," which essentially kept him from hurting himself in any manner. Occasionally he stared at the camera lens, but he did not utter a single word while his attorney jotted down notes on a pad. John Thatcher asked for a no-bail amount so that Hoffman would have to stay in jail, saying, "The weight of evidence against the defendant, well, there's no question as to his identity. He presents a flight risk due to his lack of family ties in the community other than his mother and stepfather. His unemployment and severe nature of the crime of which [he] is accused makes him a grave flight risk."

Malek, Hoffman's attorney, disagreed, saying, "Mr. Hoffman's sister and father live in northeast Ohio. He does have connections in Knox County as well. Mr. Hoffman is currently without funds, and a minimal bond with ten percent application should be set."

The hearing lasted only five minutes, and Judge Spurgeon set bail at one million dollars, an amount toward which Hoffman was unlikely to raise even the minimum amount. Judge Spurgeon also set a preliminary hearing date a little over a week away, on November 23, 2010, at which time Hoffman could enter a plea.

Sheriff Barber gave his usual afternoon press conference on November 16, and again emphasized that citizens with any information about the case should phone the sheriff's office. "We are getting a ton of calls. Tips, leads and information from the public." And once again he told the public not to touch any suspicious items but to leave them where they were so that a law enforcement officer could go and check them out.

He added, "Be assured that all that information, no matter how small it may sound, is being followed up, not only by detectives of the Knox County Sheriff's Office, but by all the other agencies as well."

Barber then showed the media photos of three vehicles he wanted the public to think about: Matthew Hoffman's silver Toyota Yaris, Tina's Ford F-150 pickup and Stephanie's Jeep. Barber said, "We want people to think back to last Wednesday or Thursday. Did you see one of these vehicles? Maybe at a restaurant, maybe parked along a road somewhere. Give us that information and let us follow up on it."

And so, as requested, tips kept coming.

Kelly P reported to authorities that a friend of hers said that her ex-husband had once lived with Matthew

Hoffman for a couple of months. Detectives found this ex-husband, who offered to let authorities search all seventy acres of his farm.

Brenda C said she'd seen a man with a young boy who looked like Kody at a buffet. The adult male was white, with a thin build and wearing a flannel shirt. Brenda took a photo of the man with her cell phone and sent it in to police.

Elissa T reported that she'd seen Stephanie Sprang's Jeep parked near Matthew Hoffman's residence quite often in the previous months. While potentially interesting information, ultimately this could not be verified.

Crystal G reported that she had been on Amity Road near dark on November 5 and had almost hit Matthew Hoffman, who she said had just been sitting in his car in the middle of the road, staring out into the cornfields.

Other potential leads came in directly to the investigators.

Detective David Light spoke with Patrolman Andy Burns of the Mount Vernon Police Department. Burns related that a man named Doug Tucker informed him that in the past August, Matthew Hoffman had been at Tucker's house for a cookout. Tucker had a large fire pit in his backyard where they were cooking, and Hoffman had allegedly commented, "This would be a good place to burn a body."

Burns said that Tucker was currently in Florida but that another friend of his had called him in the previous week and asked if he could use the fire pit to burn something. That raised the question, had Hoffman or the friend burned something related to the crime on King Beach Road in that fire pit? This was checked out, but nothing leading to the crimes was present.

Lieutenant Gary Rohler received an e-mail from a man named Joe Aldrich, who wrote that he had been friends for nine months with Matt Hoffman while both had been inmates at the Trinidad Correctional Facility in Colorado. Even after Joe was transferred to a minimum security institution, they had kept in touch by mail. At the time, Joe had considered Hoffman to be a good person who had made a stupid mistake when he burglarized and torched the condominium in Steamboat Springs.

Joe added, "I knew Matt, and he had no friends besides myself, and I don't know whether in the last five years if he had very many. I hope that you have good leads as to the location of the three missing people, hopefully alive. Matt is a very intelligent person, and very closemouthed, but I hope that he talks to you soon regarding their fate. If I can help in any way, either by possibly having some influence over getting him to open up, or giving you insight into his personality, please contact me."

A retired police officer mentioned to Lieutenant Rohler that there had been a recent fire that destroyed a business on Millersburg Road in Martinsburg, Ohio. Given Matt Hoffman's known penchant for arson, the officer wondered if the business had been inspected by an arson specialist to see if Hoffman might've been involved.

Forrest Frazee, the friend of Stephanie Sprang whom

Ron Metcalf had mentioned to police, also contacted KCSO and went to the office to write out a statement in person. Forrest wrote that Stephanie had been looking for work cleaning houses. According to Forrest, Tina told Stephanie about a job to clean a friend's place. Then a few weeks later, Stephanie and Tina went to look at a house on Columbus Road.

According to Forrest, Stephanie was to clean this house at some point, but supposedly there were plumbing issues that had to be taken care of first. Forrest believed the person whose house Stephanie was supposed to clean was Matthew Hoffman. This person's mother lived near Tina's residence, and in fact, Hoffman's mom did live nearby.

Forrest continued, "I knew this guy creeped Stephanie out. She would not meet him alone. I do know for sure that Stef and Tina did go to a Columbus Road address on a Friday sometime in the past three weeks. I know Tina was talking to this man at one time." Forrest even thought Tina might have wanted to go on a date with him but had decided against it. Forrest also wrote that he thought Tina and this man had connected on Facebook.

This brought a whole new angle to the case. Had Tina actually thought of dating Matt Hoffman and then turned him down? Was that why there was so much blood in Tina's house? Had he gone through another situation with a woman, like his ex-girlfriend, been rejected and then gone berserk? Or was this new information really off the mark?

Still, there was some more information to support the possibility that Hoffman had met Stephanie before, at least.

Detective Craig Feeney learned that Stephanie's ex-husband, Mike Sprang, had put an addition on Matt Hoffman's house a few years back, and Feeney was told that "his wife did odds and ends there also." In other words, Stephanie Sprang might actually have done some cleaning at Hoffman's residence, at some point.

This story seemed credible. Patrolman Tim Arnold of the Mount Vernon Police Department was told that Mike Sprang had also done some work on Matt Hoffman's mother's residence, and according to the informant, Stephanie had accompanied Mike on some of those jobs as well.

All of Knox County was having a hard time coming to grips with the ongoing situation. Not surprisingly, this was especially true for the schoolchildren of the area. Dr. Rick Stutzman, a psychologist who worked with the Mount Vernon Schools, said, "It evokes the number one fear for both children and parents—the loss of a child or the loss of a parent." But Stutzman encouraged parents to talk to their kids and be honest even if they didn't have all the answers. "By encouraging children to ask frank and accurate questions, we are reassuring them that the questions they have are normal and okay," he said.

Dr. Christopher Fiumera, a psychologist in Mount Vernon, agreed with Stutzman. He advised parents to "answer their [children's] questions accurately, but without speculation. Speculation can exacerbate anxiety." And Fiumera stressed that parents should reassure their children that "there are things we do as a family, or as a school group, to keep [them] safe. Talk about those things in a very reassuring way. And reassure them about the rarity of this type of crime."

Fiumera expanded upon this latter point, saying that the very rarity of this type of crime made it hard for parents to explain about what to feel and what to do. Fiumera added, "It's a unique situation that our day-to-day living skills have not schooled us in because we don't deal with it very often. But don't avoid the subject. That's the worst thing to do."

The East Knox School District, where both Sarah and Kody attended school, was feeling the weight of these events. The Ohio Crisis Response Team, some of whom had worked with survivors of the 9/11 tragedy, was working with the school district.

Sarah's and Kody's classmates at East Knox Middle School had been particularly hard hit by the situation, but School Superintendent Matthew Caputo admitted that even teachers and staff were affected. Truth be told, there was hardly a person in Knox County who wasn't.

TWENTY-TWO

"Prepare Yourself"

Sheriff David Barber closed his statements at the Tuesday, November 16, 2010, press conference by saying, "There's a ton of rumors out there right now. We can't speculate on that kind of information. Just be assured that any information received will definitely be followed up on. We're just not going to speculate as to 'Did someone do this, did someone do that?' We're not going to make up a theory." Before opening the floor to questions, he reiterated that there were certain things "I can't discuss, lab results and things like that, that would impede the investigation. I won't answer any question today that are of a speculative nature."

The first question asked was whether Matthew Hoffman was cooperating with investigators, or if his public defender had said anything that might help find the missing people. Barber replied, "Hoffman's represented by the public defender's office at this time, so our contact with him is cut off."

"Has he said anything at all?"

"Not since he's been represented."

Someone wanted to know how Sarah Maynard was doing. Barber said, "Everything that we've been told from her father is that she's doing well under the circumstances. I'm looking forward to meeting this young lady in person because she has more friends and fans than she's ever going to realize. And she is receiving services from the county."

A reporter asked what Matthew Hoffman had been wearing when he was videotaped for his court appearance. Barber explained, "That's a suicide gown," which raised the follow-up question, "Did he try to commit suicide?"

Sheriff Barber said, "He has not. But as the sheriff of the county, who is responsible for the operation of the jail, I have to comply with Ohio's minimum standards, if an inmate exhibits any behavior or any indication that they may harm themselves. It's my responsibility to protect that person from doing that. So that's why he's wearing the suicide gown."

A reporter asked, "Did he threaten to commit suicide?"

Barber began to reply, "He gave indications to the jail staff and investigators—" then cut himself off and ended with, "Well, until a mental health professional says otherwise, he'll be in the suicide gown."

The sheriff was asked if he could talk about specific areas that had been searched. To this Barber said, "A lot of the searches were centered at Foundation Park. There were some other areas around Gambier and Kenyon College. Mostly around where the pickup truck was recovered. The searches have expanded anywhere between the crime scene on King Beach Drive to where the pickup truck was found to Matthew Hoffman's house on Columbus Road. Our priority is to find Stephanie, Tina and Kody, but we also have to look for evidence that may have been left by Hoffman anywhere between King Beach Drive and his house."

A reporter asked if any significant evidence had been found so far. With all the trash bags and items of clothing found in roadside ditches and elsewhere, the reporter wondered how much the sheriff's office could take in. Barber said that all items that were deemed as possibly being connected to the case would be looked at. Then he added, "One thing we will have for you tomorrow are photographs of the clothing worn by Kody, Tina for sure, and hopefully Stephanie. Clothing they were wearing the last time anyone saw them. We're in the process of getting these photos. Most of them are from videos from the school, businesses and places where they may have been when last seen. We want to get those out to you guys in the media, so that if someone sees a hooded sweatshirt for instance somewhere"—Kody Maynard had last been seen wearing a hooded sweatshirt—"they won't think, 'Oh, that just fell out of someone's truck.'"

One reporter wanted to know if the trash bags that

had been found at Tina's residence and traced back to a Walmart were significant. Barber did not respond directly, saying, "We have recovered significant evidence in this case, but I'm not going to be specific."

"When you say 'significant,' you mean involving the young girl, or the three missing people?"

Barber replied, "The entire case."

"Can you shed any light into how Matt Hoffman got into that house and got those people under his control?"

Barber answered that it was a speculative question and not something he was going to get into.

By Tuesday, November 16, the crime tape had been removed from around Tina's residence on King Beach Drive and Greg Borders had been allowed back inside. When Tina's brothers noticed that the crime tape was gone, they called Larry Maynard about going in to retrieve belongings. Larry said later, "We had to ask Greg's permission to come inside the house, since he still owned it. He said okay, and I went in with Tina's brothers. Before I even set one foot inside, they had told me, 'Larry, prepare yourself [because they had already been inside]. Once you go in, all your questions about Tina, Kody and Stephanie are going to be answered.'

"I went inside and was absolutely shocked. I had expected some blood, but nothing like this! There was blood everywhere. On the walls, on the carpet. Large amounts of it. I had still held out hope for Tina and Kody up until then, although things didn't look good. But at that moment I knew they were dead. No one lost that amount of blood and was still alive.

"I went into Kody's room, sat down on his bed and started bawling. I couldn't stop crying. Greg was standing nearby just shaking his head. He didn't say a word. It was so weird—I was crying my eyes out and he was absolutely silent.

"I wanted to get some of Kody's things to take with me," Larry related. "Greg just said to take what I wanted, and then he left the room.

"I got Kody's shirts and clothes, especially his baseball uniforms. I also took his trophies and baseball card collection. I noticed there were candy wrappers everywhere. Kody loved candy and had stashed candy in drawers and all over the room. I picked up his PlayStation and then got the guitar I'd bought him. It was unreal. Here were all his things, but I knew he was gone.

"Sarah wanted some of her mom's clothing, especially the Dairy Queen sweatshirts she had. I got those and some of Sarah's clothes. The sheriff's office had some of Tina's jewelry. It was still evidence at that point. I didn't get much out of Sarah's room. When I was in there I noticed blood spatters on the wall and a lot of blood on the carpet. No one told me at that time, but I learned later that was where Matthew Hoffman killed Stephanie.

"I took all of these things and put them in my car. I was in a state of shock. It was like I would wake up from this and it would all be a nightmare. But I didn't wake up. It just went on and on."

* * *

Volunteers and professional teams continued to search the woods near Tina Herrmann's residence for more clues. Other teams searched along a bike path near the parking lot where Tina Herrmann's pickup truck had been found. And more unused gravel pits were searched as well. By now the Delaware County Sheriff's Office (DCSO) was also helping out on the case. They sent two dog teams with handlers to search the Kokosing Gap Trail.

The National Center for Missing and Exploited Children (NCMEC) was also giving assistance to KCSO. NCMEC Executive Director Bob Wally explained, "We provide analytical support from a center as well as mapping services for ground searches. We have some of the best resources in the country. We maintain databases where information on individuals can be shared immediately. There are also search dogs available if needed."

In addition, NCMEC offered case analysis support as well as the services of its forensic imaging unit and photo distribution division. As Wally explained, "As far as search methods and how much we are used, it's all up to the local officials. We will do as much or as little as they request."

Reporters, meanwhile, were trying to learn everything they could about Matt Hoffman, including his stint in a Colorado prison for robbery and arson at the condominium complex in Steamboat Springs. One reporter of the *Mount Vernon News* contacted attorney

Charles Feldmann, who had prosecuted Hoffman there. Feldmann said, "He just struck me as someone who had a horrific appetite, a premeditated appetite, to cause that kind of damage and the potential loss of life. You just don't see those kinds of people in small rural towns."

The *Mount Vernon News* interviewed many local townspeople, who offered their unique perspectives on the tragedy. Sandy McQuigg, who was picking up her grandson at Columbia Elementary School when stopped by the reporter, said, "In small-town America, we like to think we're still safe." In fact, this was a common theme coming from many people in the area. They could not believe that Mount Vernon and Apple Valley had become the scenes of such horrific crimes.

Seventy-two-year-old Ted Dingler recounted how the sermon at his church on Sunday had been changed by the pastor to reflect on the incident. The pastor had asked the congregation to meditate and pray for the missing. Dingler declared that you could have heard a pin drop in the church.

Even at the public library, the situation was on everyone's minds. Employees were gathered around a television, watching the news. Krista Smith, whose daughter went to school with Sarah, said, "We're all glued to the television in hopes of finding out why this happened." On a window at the Dairy Queen where Tina worked, a sign stating "Pray for our missing families" had replaced the daily specials.

Journalists spoke to Hoffman's former supervisor at

Fast Eddy's grounds-keeping and tree-trimming service, Sandy Burd, who recounted how Hoffman seemed like a normal guy at first but then became increasingly strange. "He would just stare into space. And he oversold his tree-trimming experience," she told them. Richard Burch, of Burch Tree Care, related that Matthew Hoffman had worked for him as a tree-trimmer from October 28 through November 3. Burch said he was aware that Hoffman drove two different vehicles, the silver Yaris and a red Dodge Neon. Burch added, "Matthew is very knowledgeable with trees and ropes, and he always had several rolls of rope in the Yaris."

The newspapers published information from the police report filed October 24, 2010, by Hoffman's former girlfriend, in which she described Hoffman pushing her to the floor and choking her. That incident occurred only seventeen days before the crimes at Tina Herrmann's residence.

Reporters once again spoke with Matt Hoffman's neighbor, Dawna Davis. She repeated some of the things she'd said to the media before, and added that the whole situation was "crazy." She said that Hoffman had "seemed like a decent guy at first." And then she reiterated how he had become very "weird" in her estimation.

Ron Fowler, Dawna's live-in boyfriend, related, "He was really weird about the squirrels. We were feeding them and he killed them!" Ron also noted Hoffman's affinity for trees. "He was an athletic guy and he'd climb up into those trees."

As to the present circumstances, Ron said, "I saw him on Friday [November 12] with his backpack walking towards the old gravel pit in Foundation Park. It was an area he knew well. My son even went swimming in that gravel pit with him."

Dawna said that she had seen Hoffman poking around in his backyard fire pit one night the previous week. She added, "I feel so bad that I was right here and didn't hear anything . . . That basement where [Sarah] was, it was so dark and dirty that Hoffman's girlfriend wouldn't let the dog down there. And the worst thing was, I went outside that week and would shout my daughter's name. Her name is Sarah too. I might have given Sarah Maynard false hope. Every time I yelled for my daughter, Sarah Maynard probably thought someone was going to help her."

Stephanie Sprang's father, Stephen Thompson, went on WBNS TV and said that the family still held out hope for the rescue of the three missing people. Stephen stated, "If Stephanie can hear us out there, I want her to know, and hopefully she can feel our thoughts, that we will get her back. Your mom, me, your whole family—we're all looking for you."

Stephen added that the entire situation was beyond comprehension and they barely knew how to cope with it, other than to keep searching for Stephanie and hope that she was still alive.

Tip after tip barraged the KCSO phone lines, and they all had to be taken into consideration.

Duct-taped trash bags were discovered by a volunteer alongside a road in eastern Knox County, about a half mile from where Tina Herrmann's pickup truck had been located by Officer Aaron Phillips, and where he had also spotted Matthew Hoffman sitting in his Toyota Yaris. Though duct-taped trash bags were suspicious under the circumstances, nothing ultimately came of the finding.

Selena R called in to report that her uncle used to work with Hoffman. Supposedly Hoffman had said at one time, "Small's Sand and Gravel would be a good place to put bodies." Officers went to Small's, a local construction materials company, to check out the lead, but no bodies were discovered there.

A woman who would not give her name phoned KCSO and said that a lot on the 900 block of High Street in Mount Vernon needed to be checked. According to this woman, Hoffman had a treehouse there and it was filled with tools and other equipment.

Another tipster reported, "I was stopped by a female in Grand Island, Nebraska, seeking money for gas. She was travelling with a mother and son. I asked her destination and she said it was Colorado." This brought up the remote possibility that Matt Hoffman had a female accomplice who was taking Tina and Kody to Colorado.

Tiffany S said, "At the spillway on Knox Lake, off of Woodview Lane, there are three trash bags. One has a shoe sticking out of it." Another person reported that something blue could be seen in the water of the nearby lake. And she indicated that the something blue might be an article of clothing.

Kim P related that she had a friend who used to date Matthew Hoffman, and gave authorities the name. She also said that a man nicknamed Opie used to hang around with Hoffman a lot.

A man named Fred declared that he had passed a Toyota Yaris with a dent off of Harcourt and Columbus Road on Thursday morning, November 11, between 7:00 and 7:30 AM.

In the realm of intriguing but ultimately useless information, a man who would not give his name declared that he worked at a barber shop in Mount Vernon and a customer recently came in and wanted to give him a knife that he'd found in the Walmart parking lot. This caller said there had possibly been blood on the knife and that he didn't want it. The caller didn't know who the man was who wanted to give him the knife, and had no idea of where that person or the knife might be now. All the investigators inquiries about this alleged knife got nowhere, and most likely was not part of the crime scene on King Beach Drive.

Greg V reported that near a small waterfall on Magers Road he'd found a bloody surgical glove.

Patty K related that a man on High Street named Carl was friends with Matt Hoffman, and that the two men had been up in trees on Carl's place many times. Hoffman had even created a pulley system in the tree so items could be hauled up into the branches.

Aaron P related that he used to party with Matt Hoffman. This had been on Caves Road near some waterfalls. A K-9 team was sent to that area, but they found nothing related to the crime.

On Wednesday, November 17, Debra Hawkins contacted Lieutenant Gary Rohler and said that she worked in corrections. She had a theory that if Sarah hadn't been sexually assaulted (she had been, but that news had not been released to the media yet), that perhaps the suspect had been holding her to be sold later into the sex-slave trade. Debra related that if that was the case, "more people are involved." She added, "Being a mother, I know that I would have put up one hell of a fight to protect my children." Debra surmised that was why there had been so much blood in Tina's residence.

Bryant G said that he had once lived next to Matt Hoffman on Columbus Road and that they'd gone a lot of places together. One of those places was Wolf Run. "Matt was just a very strange person," Bryant said, mentioning that Hoffman had had a frequent male visitor who drove "a Toyota 4Runner, gray or light blue in color." It was "a 1990s model." More important, Bryant said he had seen Tina's Ford pickup truck near Hoffman's residence on Wednesday night, November 10, at around 11 PM. It had been parked in the alley in back of Hoffman's residence. Either Wednesday or Thursday night, Bryant had seen Hoffman out in back of his house near a fire in the backyard. Just why Bryant had seen all this activity, he didn't say in his tip.

A call from another tipster, Brian F, seemed to corroborate Bryant's claim that Tina's truck had been parked at Hoffman's place. Brian told authorities that one of his coworkers lived next to Hoffman, and this person had seen Tina's pickup parked next to Hoffman's place on Wednesday, November 10. This made investigators wonder if Hoffman had taken the truck there at some point after he'd entered Tina's home and kidnapped Sarah.

Todd K related that he had seen Hoffman in Dutch's Bar on Tuesday night, November 9. It had been late at night, and Todd had said, "What's up?" Hoffman replied, "Not much." Hoffman stayed only five minutes or so. When he was leaving, Todd said to him, "I'll see you later," to which Hoffman replied, "No, you won't." Todd added, "He was a weird individual." Todd also stated that he'd seen Hoffman's silver Yaris with a dent in an alley off of Pleasant Street, two times between 2:00 and 3:00 AM on Wednesday, November 10. There had been a single occupant in the car wearing a hoodie and a ball cap.

A woman who would give her name only as Melissa said that Tina always wore a sixteen-inch diamond-cut chain with a dolphin attached. The dolphin was a yellow- and rose-gold charm, and she never took it off.

Detective Sergeant Roger Brown and BCI&I Special Agent Gary Wilgus went to the East Knox Middle School and examined Kody's and Sarah's lockers. They secured evidence from both lockers for DNA purposes. They also spoke with the school's information technology manager about the school's surveillance video for November 10, 2010.

Ron Metcalf, Stephanie's boyfriend, said he had received a text from someone claiming that Stephanie had been seen with Matt Hoffman buying plumbing products. The person who texted him could not recall the date or time.

TWENTY-THREE

The Hunt for a Miracle

On-the-ground searches continued apace on Wednesday, November 17, 2010. One five-man team consisted of volunteers who had skills in tracking and search and rescue. These men came from Bucyrus, Delaware, and Marion, Ohio, towns far afield of Apple Valley. One of the men, Jon Reed, said, "We did not come looking to find bodies. We just wanted to help look for clues. Especially near water areas where someone could easily place a person or a body. We searched around the bike path and the Brown Family Environmental Center. We also went out to the quarry."

They searched the area around Small's Sand and Gravel near Gambier, because apparently Matthew Hoffman had worked there at one time. Reed explained, "We found some trash and a couple of old shoes—nothing fresh. You look for things like drag marks, tire tracks or freshly moved dirt in wild settings. If I was in the same situation, I'd want a million people out searching for my family."

Despite the fact that Jon Reed said the volunteers weren't searching for bodies, a headline in the *Mount Vernon News* summed up the feeling of many on November 17:

HOPE FADES AS TIMES PASSES

The reporter noted that even Sheriff David Barber sounded more pessimistic than before, and his Wednesday news conference lasted only ten minutes.

"A lot of sightings and information have been received by the sheriff's office and continue to be followed up by not only our investigators, but by BCI&I, the FBI and other outside agencies. These tips and leads have yielded some information that is helpful to the investigation. A lot of it has just been citizens being very conscientious and trying to be helpful, which we appreciate, and we want them to continue giving us information and leads.

"I told you yesterday that we were going to have photographs of the last known clothing that Tina, Kody and Stephanie were wearing. Unfortunately when you look at the video—we could tell what it was, but they didn't reproduce well. So I'm just going to give you what clothing descriptions we have. We know for sure what Tina Herrmann was wearing last Wednesday. It was a white baseball cap, a tan hoodie, dark-colored sweatpants and tennis shoes.

"As far as Kody Maynard goes, [he] was wearing black shoes, jeans, a gray T-shirt and a blue zip-up hoodie. We're still trying to find information about what Stephanie was wearing.

"We did get some responses about the photos of the vehicles that were put out, which will add a little more detail to our timeline. Other than that, the investigation is progressing, and unfortunately the reality that these folks may not be alive is becoming more and more prevalent, simply because there's been no word from these folks. There's been no credit card activity, no cell phone activity [or] anything like that since this event occurred.

"Evidence is being submitted to BCI&I for evaluation and analysis. We have been assured that the submissions in this investigation are priorities for BCI&I. I will take just a few questions since there are a lot of things going on."

A reporter asked what Sarah had said about Matthew Hoffman and what his relationship might have been with the missing people. Barber answered, "It's inappropriate for me to discuss anything Sarah has said to us."

Another media person wanted to know if Hoffman had had a preset plan to kidnap or attack any of these four people. Barber replied, "We follow the investigation where it leads us, and that's yet to be determined."

Turning the focus from the victims to the investigators, one person queried, "What has been the emotional toll on you and your staff as you go through this ordeal?"

Barber responded, "It's been a challenge because we have been blessed in this county—we've never had to respond to something this major and this involved. I cannot say enough about the overwhelming support we've had with all our partners in this investigation. As the sheriff of Knox County, I am not territorial, I don't think that I'm so big and know it all that I would ever try to handle an event and investigation this big by myself. I'm proud to ask for help. All of this has definitely been a challenge for us and our families."

Another headline also captured the mood of the day:

CITIZENS GETTING FRUSTRATED AS THEY HUNT FOR A MIRACLE

The reporter had spoken to several search volunteers. One of these volunteers, Cindy McBride, told the reporter, "It's not that I don't want to have hope. But it's been seven days now, and it's scary."

A woman named Debbie Henthorn was just one of many people spreading the word online about the case and its impact on the region. She noted that she had moved to Mount Vernon almost thirty years earlier, and enjoyed its small-town feeling. She described it as the kind of place where you knew your neighbors and the person who bagged your groceries at the local market.

Debbie said that she, like many in the community,

had held her breath when there was live coverage of a car being pulled out of a pond at Foundation Park. When it was determined that the car was unconnected to the case, "a sigh of relief went up [in my office] only to be deflated once again knowing that Tina, Kody and Stephanie were still missing."

Debbie also noted that in a recent football game, the Blue Devils of Danville were going up against their rival, the East Knox Bulldogs. Both Sarah and Kody were students in the East Knox School System. Despite the usually heated rivalry, even the Danville players were wearing the color purple, to honor Sarah and Kody.

Debbie wrote, "This is how small towns react in the face of tragedy. They help in any way they can. Strangers console one another. They pray alone or together. We give each other hope, no matter how dark things seem. And I can't imagine living in any different type of community."

Knox County Emergency Management Agency (EMA) Director Brian Hess was doing all he could to coordinate the search volunteers. He encouraged the volunteers to meet at the parking lot of the Premiere Theatres in Mount Vernon. A Red Cross unit there would then give the different teams instructions.

Volunteers had found two sweatshirts, one blue and one purple, that were being processed by authorities. They were a boy's size, and Kody had been seen wearing a blue sweatshirt when he came home on the day he and Sarah were attacked.

Near the town of Gambier, volunteer Jim Fletcher wore an orange hunting vest and overalls, and was bundled up against the chilly rain. For over six hours he scoured woods, fields and fence lines astride his all-terrain vehicle. He said, "We're looking everywhere we can think of. We want to find them, but we're running out of places to look."

Volunteers were also using a Facebook page, "Pray for the Maynard Kids," to coordinate search efforts. Jennifer Kessler, who knew Tina, Kody and Sarah, was using the page to coordinate efforts in the Apple Valley area. On the previous evening, the page had seventy-seven hundred followers. Many of them had changed their own profile photo to one that symbolized the missing three individuals—three lighted candles. One posting stated, "Okay, Lord, we need a miracle now."

More tipsters contacted investigators:

Beth B contacted KCSO saying that they might want to check out a hollow tree in the woods off of Maplewood Avenue.

Carl P stated that he was a friend of Hoffman's and knew that Hoffman would sometimes go to the drainage ponds that were between Walmart and Staples.

Debbie M said she had been working at a residence across the street from Hoffman's place on Columbus Road in the previous week. She thought she saw him take a baby carrier into his house.

Mike H said he'd been out around 6:45 AM on Tues-

day, November 9. He thought he'd seen a car like Hoffman's silver Yaris parked close to a lot near a business
called Noff's.

Charles W, meanwhile, was sure that on the previous
Tuesday he'd seen Hoffman in a Lowe's parking lot with
a woman who had long blond hair.

Another tipster, Nora G, related, "On November 3, I
was at Kmart around 4:45 PM and parked beside a small
silver car with a dent. The car had trash bags piled up in
the backseat and a blue tarp. In the store, there was a
male who looked like Matt Hoffman. He was with another male about six-foot-one who had dark hair, and
was of medium build."

Thomas C left a message that on Sunday or Monday,
November 7 or 8, he'd seen a black van drive by Tina Herrmann's house very slowly. Someone knocked on the
door, but when Tina went to answer, the person ran into
the woods. Around the same time, Thomas said, "Stephanie heard footsteps in the garage of Tina's house." Supposedly Thomas knew Stephanie and she had told him
this. Whether it was true or not, the investigators were
not able to verify this. If it was true, it indicated that Hoffmann, or someone else might have been casing Tina's
house before the crimes of November 10th.

Bobbi H contacted KCSO and related that "Stephanie
had a tracking device on her phone," meaning that if
Matt Hoffman had taken her phone and used it, the area
where he used it could be traced.

James B told KCSO, "Driving by the Kokosing Dam
at two in the morning on Wednesday [November 10], I

saw a man leaving the woods with a dog. He was using a flashlight."

And yet another man who would not give his name declared, "I just thought the coverage of the Elizabeth Smart trial in Utah might set Hoffman off, and get him to talk." This trial concerned a deranged man and his accomplice kidnapping a young blond girl in Utah. Elizabeth Smart, like Sarah, survived and eventually regained her freedom.

Louis R believed the bodies were "in an old barn somewhere." The only problem with that tip was, there were a lot of old barns in that part of Ohio.

Despite their weakening hope, volunteers were still pouring in. Between three hundred and four hundred people congregated at the KCSO headquarters at the request of the sheriff's office, where EMA Director Brian Hess was in charge of coordinating the various teams. Each team was assigned a specific location, with most of the teams being sent out to the Apple Valley and Gambier portions of the county. All of this activity occurred during November 17th.

Hess put into action a grid-pattern searching system, a much more effective search method than the random one used in the earlier volunteer efforts. The search teams would now search in a grid pattern, which would ensure they didn't overlook some areas or search the same areas twice. Hess told one reporter, "Today's turnout is a great testament of the people of Knox County."

The miles of rivers, creeks and ponds in the Apple Valley area made the searches difficult at best. A pair of kayakers volunteered to row down one of the rivers looking for anything that might be pertinent to the case. Others thrashed through undergrowth and brambles.

In an effort to provide a broader perspective on cases like the one unfolding in Apple Valley, the *Mount Vernon News* contacted Jack Levin, codirector of the Brudnick Center on Violence and Conflict at Northeastern University in Boston. Levin, an expert on such situations, said that Sarah Maynard was "very, very lucky to be alive. When a stranger abducts a girl, the kidnapper almost always acts alone." He also said that while there were about 58,000 child abductions in the United States per year, almost all of those were by parents or relatives of the children. There had been only 115 stranger kidnappings of children in the previous year. "Sometimes a group will attack a family in a random act of violence, but those cases are rare, and the situation in Knox County doesn't seem to fit that pattern."

Levin also said that in most violent cases that involved families, the bodies were generally left at the scene of the crime. He did note that in crimes where an individual acted alone, the assailant was generally someone who had lost their job and broken up in a relationship not long before the crime.

In Matthew Hoffman's case, both were true.

TWENTY-FOUR

The Hollow Tree

Aside from his strange bathroom conference with BCI&I Special Agent Joe Dietz, Matthew Hoffman had been as silent as a sphinx since his arrest on the morning of November 14, 2010. But there were changes in the air by the end of the day on November 17. Behind the scenes, even as tips continued to come in and searchers fanned out throughout the community, Prosecutor John Thatcher had started working out a deal with Matthew Hoffman and his attorney.

Hoffman had told Special Agent Dietz on November 15 that he wanted to die; he wanted Dietz to arrange a situation where Hoffman could appear to attempt an escape and then be shot dead. By late November 17, however, Hoffman seemed to have lost his interest in dying. In fact, in exchange for the prosecutor's taking the death penalty off the table, he agreed to tell authorities where he'd hidden the bodies of Tina Herrmann, Kody Maynard and Stephanie Sprang.

Before any legal documents could be signed with Hoffman and his attorneys, Prosecutor Thatcher met with the victims' closest relatives. Even though the final judgment was his, Thatcher wanted them to know what was happening and allow them to give their input.

Several people were initially against Matthew Hoffman being allowed to escape the death penalty. But Thatcher convinced them that making this deal was their only real means of finding their loved ones' remains. Otherwise, Tina, Kody and Stephanie might not be found for years, if ever. Eventually all agreed that this was the best they could hope for.

After the meeting, Thatcher began writing up the all-important agreement for Hoffman and his attorneys to sign. The first stipulation on the list was that the prosecutor's office would not seek the death penalty if "all conditions were met." Second was that Hoffman would lead investigators to the remains of Tina, Kody and Stephanie within twenty-four hours of the acceptance of the agreement. Third was that all remains would be found, except for those that might have been moved by "animal activity."

The fourth point was that Hoffman had to give the Knox County Sheriff's Office a full written statement, dictated to his attorneys, including written responses to questions submitted by KCSO. Fifth was that Hoffman would plead guilty to the charges of aggravated murder, burglary, tampering with evidence, abuse of a corpse, kidnapping and sexual assault. Sixth on the list was that the State of Ohio and the defense would jointly recommend to the judge a prison sentence of life without parole.

After consultation among all the would-be signatories, the document was signed by Prosecutor John Thatcher, Matthew Hoffman, Sheriff David Barber, and Hoffman's public defenders, who now included not only Bruce Malek but also assistant public defenders Brandon Crunkilton and Fred Mayhew.

Detective David Light later noted, "On Thursday, November 18, 2010, Matthew Hoffman and his attorneys reached an agreement with Knox County Prosecutor John Thatcher, to reveal where the bodies of Tina Herrmann, Kody Maynard and Stephanie Sprang were located. Hoffman disclosed the location through his attorneys."

In essence, Matthew Hoffman wasn't going to accompany investigators to the location, but would give them directions to the spot.

Unaware that Hoffman had struck a deal with the prosecutor, volunteer searchers continued to comb woods, fields and stream banks. Even if they had known, perhaps they would have continued anyway; there was always the possibility that Hoffman could've been lying.

About three hundred volunteers gathered at the Premier Theatres parking lot on Thursday morning, November 18, to be assigned their tasks for the day ahead.

This was the third day of coordinated searching. It was a very cold, blustery day. Many volunteers had accepted the likelihood that the missing trio would not be found alive. Still, they persisted in the search. As volunteer Charles Christopher, a student at Central Ohio Technical College put it, "I came out to help no matter what." Many of the volunteers were off-duty police officers, fire-fighters, EMT workers and even a mounted search team from surrounding counties and communities. For some of them it was the second or third day of volunteering. At the KCSO headquarters, eighty canine officers with their dogs were briefed by Deputy EMA Director Matt Sturgeon.

Volunteers were warned that the weather would be very cold and that in some places they'd be working in rough terrain. They were also told to take their time and be careful. And once again, they were instructed that if they found anything that looked like it might be related to the case, not to touch it but to call KCSO so an officer could come out and collect the item.

Doug McLaman, operations manager of the Knox County Park District, commented about the volunteers, "This is what makes Knox County unique, is that we have so many people willing to come out when the weather's like this."

To assist and support the searchers, various area res-taurants were donating coffee and snacks, and other vol-unteers supplied homemade sandwiches. Among the latter group was Brittany Peck of Mount Vernon, who said, "We came to help out all these searchers that are freezing. Many of them have come out to help someone they don't even know."

Before noon on November 18, the news of the plea deal's imminent signing reached investigators. Detective Sergeant Roger Brown recalled, "I was advised that Matthew Hoffman agreed to disclose the location of the bodies of Tina Herrmann, Kody Maynard and Stephanie Sprang. Lt. Kohler and I followed Knox County Assistant Public Defender Brandon Crunkilton, Knox County Public Defender's Office Investigator Avery Dyer and Special Agent Dietz to the Kokosing Wildlife Area on Yankee Street, Fredericktown, Ohio." This was about eight miles north of Mount Vernon.

Around the same time, Agent Joe Dietz met with other BCI&I agents at the Knox County Sheriff's Office. He told them that all the families had signed off on the deal put together by the prosecution and defense, where in exchange for taking the death penalty off the table, Matt Hoffman would disclose where the bodies of Tina, Kody and Stephanie could be found.

Dietz later recapped in his report the meeting with Hoffman's defense team, "I met with Assistant Knox County Public Defender Brandon Crunkilton and Public Defender's Office Investigator Avery Dyer. Mr. Crunkilton advised that he had received information from Matthew Hoffman as to the location of the missing victims and wanted to check the location to verify the accuracy of the information he was given. I then rode with Mr. Crunkilton and Mr. Dyer in their vehicle to locate the place where the bodies of Tina Herrmann, Kody Maynard and Stephanie Sprang were located."

Dietz documented that Lieutenant Rohler and Detective Sergeant Brown were following them in a separate vehicle. Dyer drove to a wooded area of public land in the Kokosing Lake Wildlife Area in the Yankee Street and Waterford Road locale outside of Fredericktown, Ohio; this was the area that Hoffman had indicated they should go.

Lieutenant Rohler picked up the narrative. "As we were pulling in to the wildlife area, an officer with the Ohio Department of Natural Resources, Division of Wildlife, flagged us down. Sergeant Brown explained to the officer the situation, and the Wildlife Officer was shown the map that was provided by Matthew Hoffman."

Luckily, the wildlife officer was very familiar with the area and explained in detail to the others how to get to the location that Hoffman had indicated. Without his help, the exact spot might have been very difficult to find, since to the investigators one tree looked very much like another in the area.

Detective Light, who had come on the trip as well as the others, continued, "Officers had to drive the winding path for approximately one half mile, then walk into the woods a short distance." There they found what they were looking for: "A tree with a large opening, approximately thirty to forty feet up was pointed out."

It was actually Public Defender Avery Dyer who first spotted the tree in question. It was a beech tree with a large hole about forty feet off the ground, as Detective Light described.

Special Agent Dietz noted, "The tree was approximately seventy feet tall and had obviously living branches and leaves at the top. Mr. Crunkilton indicated based on information provided to him by Mathew Hoffman that the beech tree was the likely location of the missing victims' bodies. The tree was solid and intact, although approximately forty to fifty feet above the ground, the main section of trunk divided and a large opening was visible. This opening appeared to provide access to the main trunk of the tree which appeared to be hollow."

At this point, Dyer knelt down so that Special Agent Dietz could stand on Dyer's back and peek into a small hole more than five feet off the ground. This was a separate hole from the much larger one forty feet off the ground. With the aid of a flashlight, Dietz was able to confirm that the tree was indeed hollow, with an interior space of about thirty inches in diameter.

The interior was littered with bark chips, but Dietz could also make out three small sections of plastic bag material, which appeared to be similar to the trash bags Matthew Hoffman had purchased.

It appeared that Hoffman had led them to the right place.

At that point, crime scene agents Ed Lulla, Gary Wilgus and George Staley were called to the scene. The Ohio

BCI&I special agents had been told to standby at the Knox County Sheriff's Office until the other agents located the tree. Around 1:00 PM, they got the call that the tree with the plastic trash bags had been found. The agents headed out immediately and arrived at the scene around 1:50 PM.

Once there, the trio of BCI&I agents were briefed by the others, and began their precise measurements. The beech tree was eleven feet, six inches in diameter near its base, and thirty feet up to its lowest branch. From there, it extended approximately another thirty feet up to its crown. Special Agent Staley stood next to the tree to provide scale as another agent photographed the tree. Staley was dwarfed by the large beech tree.

The small opening into which Agent Dietz had peered measured three inches wide by six inches tall, and was located five feet, six inches off the ground. A professional tree trimmer was called to the scene to make the actual cuts into the tree, as the agents did not want to accidentally harm the evidence in any way. The tree expert was a man named Jan Laymon.

Once Laymon arrived on scene, the agents and investigators stood nearby while he started making his cuts with a chain saw. After there was a wide enough opening, Special Agent Wilgus began to remove the plastic bags from the interior of the tree. He noted, "Due to their location deep inside the tree, two additional cuts in the tree had to be made to reach all of the plastic bags."

Lieutenant Rohler continued, "Special Agent Gary

Wilgus carefully and respectfully removed the large trash bags from the hollow beech tree and placed them on a tarp. Numerous garbage bags were removed."

Detective Sergeant Roger Brown added, "The agents removed the trash bags from the tree as I took photographs" of the gruesome contents, which Special Agent Wilgus confirmed "contained various dismembered body parts including the heads of Kody Maynard, Stephanie Sprang and Tina Herrmann. The remains of a small dog was also found inside one of the garbage bags, along with bloodstained towels, clothing, a hat and shoes. Upon examining the backs and torsos [of the victims], numerous deep lacerations were observed."

At some point later, Knox County Coroner Jennifer Ogle arrived on scene and the trash bags were opened for her inspection. Once all the garbage bags had been opened and the body parts identified, they were placed in official-issue body bags and released to employees of Snyder Funeral Homes to be transported to the Licking County Coroner's Office for autopsies. The Licking County Coroner's Office would be aasisting Ogle in her task.

TWENTY-FIVE

"My Heart Is So Heavy"

The news of the discovery of the bodies in the tree had, of course, hit the victims' families the hardest. Tracy Herrmann, the wife of Tina's brother Jason, later spoke of how she broke the news to her children. "I had both kids on my lap and held them while I told them the news. Madison, my eight-year-old, was crying and I was full of tears. My five-year-old, Alex's, little bottom lip quivered but he refused to cry. He just kept wiping my tears, trying to stay strong for Mommy and his sister.

"I know that Kody was protective of his sister, Sarah, too," Tracy said. "They had a close bond, and Sarah had even written Kody a note for his lunch the day they went to school for the last time, telling him how proud of him she was. I am sure both kids were brave and fought all they could for each other. Against Matthew Hoffman they didn't have a chance."

Lisa Robey, the girlfriend of Tina's brother Bill, asked a question that was on many people's minds: "Why?" Why had Matthew Hoffman chosen to kill and dismember these three individuals? She added, "It is a question that has no answer, because no answer will ever be good enough. And no answer will ever change what happened. All we can do is turn this one over to God and pray. We pray that Sarah will be able to once again find precious love for herself that every girl needs. And will someday be able to hold her head high and grow into the beautiful strong woman we all know she is destined to be."

Stephanie's father, Steve Thompson, would later say, "My heart is so heavy, my mind is blank. My trust in everyone is shaken. I know my daughter is at peace, and I'm glad that she doesn't have to see the change in all of us."

By 5:00 PM on the evening of Thursday, November 18, it was finally time to share with the world the sad news regarding what had befallen Tina Herrmann, Kody Maynard and Stephanie Sprang. Sheriff David Barber held another news conference, sounding tired and saddened by the turn of events. Barber began by saying, "It's been a long week for Knox County and this community. It's been a long week for the families of Sarah, Kody, Tina and Stephanie. Today, this investigation took a major turn. We have discovered the remains of Kody Maynard, Stephanie Sprang and Tina Herrmann.

"The discovery of those bodies was the result of information produced by Matthew Hoffmann. The bodies were located in a wooded area inside garbage bags in a hollow tree off of Yankee Street, which is not far from Fredericktown here in Knox County." He went on to say that the three recovered bodies had been turned over to the Knox County Coroner, and to assure people that Hoffman remained in the county jail.

Barber also took the time to thank his fellow law enforcement agencies. "It's been a long week, a very stressful week, for this entire county and particularly for law enforcement. My office could not have come to the point we are at today but for the outstanding assistance provided by the Federal Bureau of Investigation, the Ohio Attorney General's Office, BCI&I, the Ohio State Highway Patrol, the Mount Vernon Police Department, the Franklin County Sheriff's Office, the Delaware County Sheriff's Office, the Central Ohio Child Abduction Response Team and the tremendous amount of volunteers that we had.

"As the sheriff of this county for eighteen years, I have never experienced a case this big and this tragic. And in my entire law enforcement career I have never experienced anything like this. It's reassuring to know that when something like this happens, and God forbid we should ever have to go through anything like this again, that I can depend upon all the agencies and then some. There were even more people waiting in the wings to help out with this tragedy.

"There's a lot more to be done in this case. We were

optimistic a few days ago that there was a remote chance that these folks were still alive. This is a homicide investigation now. It is the homicide of three individuals. As the homicide investigation progresses, it will be turned over to the Knox County Prosecutor's Office."

At that, Sheriff Barber stepped aside and Prosecutor John Thatcher began to address the media. He said, "As happy as we were with Sarah's rescue on Sunday, we have to deal with this tragedy now. I want to express my deepest condolences to the Maynard, Herrmann and Sprang families. I also want to express my gratitude to all the people who helped in the searches. It was a phenomenal thing to watch. I want to keep Sarah in my prayers and hope that she can recover and overcome this.

"As the sheriff said, this investigation is ongoing. I've been able to be involved in the investigation—and as it continues, I'm sure it will be an excellent job, as was done in the last week. When I get the final report from the law enforcement agencies, and there's been time in the prosecutor's office to analyze all the evidence, we'll review that and prepare an indictment, containing additional charges. Then we'll present that to a grand jury within the next four to six weeks. At this time I can't speculate on what those charges might be without knowing what the evidence is."

After reminding journalists that Matthew Hoffman was still being held in jail on a one-million-dollar bond and that a preliminary hearing would be held the following Tuesday, Thatcher threw the floor open to questions. The first one was prescient: a reporter asked, "Was the death penalty ever on the table and used as a tool to get a confession? In other words, 'We will take the death penalty of the table if you tell us where those folks are?'"

Thatcher did not want to discuss this aspect at that point and said, "One thing I cannot comment on is whether any such deal took place."

Another person wanted to know the timeline by which Hoffman had gotten word to the authorities about the remains. Sheriff Barber answered, "As far as the timeline goes, we received information through Matthew Hoffman's attorney early today where the victims' remains were located."

A reporter asked whether the families of the victims had been kept in the loop about the developments. Barber replied, "We have kept the families in the loop. When the case took the direction that it was headed today, we contacted them with crime victim advocates for all the families. The Knox County Sheriff's Office and all the agencies—we express our deepest condolences to the families.

"We're a small community here, and we became close to the victims' families. We have to look out for the needs of the survivors. That was part of the reason we needed to go in the direction we headed in today. At least these three families know that they've been found. They're not missing anymore. And at least the process of resolution can now start for them."

A reporter wanted to know what condition the bodies had been found in.

Barber would not describe the condition of the bodies, but said only that they had been inside trash bags and placed inside a hollow tree.

"Did this have anything to do with Matt Hoffman being a tree trimmer?"

Barber replied that called for speculation, and he would not go into that.

"Were the victims' bodies covered with the same clothing that you had mentioned them wearing the other day?"

"Yes, they were."

"Is Hoffman the only suspect right now?" Barber confirmed that he was and said there was no indication that anyone else had been involved.

Someone asked if Barber had yet met with Sarah. He said, "We did not meet with her this morning, but rather with her father and stepmother."

"How did they react?"

"I think there was a certain sense of relief. And grief as well, because they hoped it would turn out differently than the way it did. I can say that my staff and I are inspired by Sarah. We're inspired by Sarah's bravery. After we met with the families this morning, I asked Larry Maynard to convey to Sarah that she was my hero."

Another question was, "Did all the murders happen in Tina Herrmann's home?"

Barber responded, "I would say, yes."

A follow-up question was, "So, Sarah was there when the murders occurred?"

"What she saw, I can't speak to that."

"Did the victims appear to be bound in any way?"

"No."

In answer to a question about how specific Matthew Hoffman's instructions had been to get to the hollow tree, Barber said, "They were specific—we didn't have to do much searching."

At that point the press conference ended. One of the reporters said in a loud voice, "Thank you, Sheriff. Good job."

After the press conference, the news flashed throughout the community that the bodies of Tina Herrmann, Kody Maynard and Stephanie Sprang had been found. The *Mount Vernon News* ran a special announcement on their website at 5:55 PM: "Bodies Recovered."

A WBNS News helicopter had been the first to follow investigators to the Kokosing Lake Wildlife Area and film footage from above the tree line. Then the helicopter news team spotted three white hearses being driven to the area. The image of the three white hearses in the woods was a very powerful one, one that would remain for a long time in many people's minds.

On the ground, a Fredericktown woman visiting her parents told a WBNS reporter that KCSO deputies had blocked the road at the intersection of Yankee Street and Quaker Road. The woman told the reporter, "Typically, this is a very quiet and very serene area." She added that her mother had not seen any suspicious activity in the area in the last week, but that it was a very heavily wooded terrain.

Most of the people in the area realized something was happening because of the television news helicopters hovering over the wooded area. Some residents said that in the immediate community, it was more likely to see Amish passing by in their horse-drawn buggies than police activity. All said it was generally a quiet area, and many were shocked that Matt Hoffman had chosen those woods as the hiding place for the bodies.

One woman said, "I've been praying for them, but now it's just terrifying that he was this close." Another area resident said much the same, adding, "I just don't understand who could do something like this to women and a child."

TWENTY-SIX

"Our Entire Community Has Been Wounded"

The *Columbus Dispatch* of November 19th ran an article that stated, "The discovery of the bodies north of Fredericktown severed the last thin thread of hope among some community residents that the missing still might be alive, although authorities increasingly had counseled against that belief."

The newspaper also related how some people who knew Matthew Hoffman described him as an experienced outdoorsman who felt at home in the woods. One former friend even said that "Matt camped out for months in the woods before buying his home."

Trying to learn more about Matthew Hoffman, the newspaper sent a reporter out to talk to as many people as he could find about Hoffman's life. One friend, who wished to remain anonymous, said that Hoffman was intelligent "but did not have a lick of common sense." The friend added that Hoffman was very strong and liked to embrace risk; for example, once during a parade, as a large truck moved slowly down the street, Hoffman had dashed from the curb and ran beneath the truck's bed, near its moving wheels, as bystanders looked on in disbelief. This friend also described Hoffman as a tight-wad who was reluctant to spend the money he made as a tree trimmer.

Taylor Ackley, who was a little younger than Hoffman and lived down the street from him, agreed that he was "kind of strange." Ackley, however, was amazed that Hoffman had done the things he was accused of doing. Ackley said, "We'd see him out and about, climbing trees with the kids next door. They [Hoffman and his girl-friend] always left their back door open, and there would be kids running in and out."

Nicole Martin, age sixteen, lived two doors away from Hoffman and had spent summer afternoons in 2010 climbing trees with Hoffman and the other kids and swinging on ropes he tied to tree branches. She did admit to the reporter, "He was weird. It's just weird he could be next door and do something so horrible."

About this weird quality in Hoffman, his anonymous friend related, "The guy was kind off, a little weird, but I chalked a lot of it up to being in prison. I can't fathom him killing anyone, but something had to have snapped. Maybe he's living in a fantasy world, stuck in his imagi-nation. I sense that he is happy with the outcome, that he caused turmoil and is infamous."

* * *

Among those with very little to say at that point was Knox County Coroner Jennifer Ogle, who would be doing the autopsies of the three victims. She did tell reporters, "We will work closely with the investigation team to provide information that will lead to the prosecution of this assault in our community. As a mother and a resident, my heart breaks for Sarah and the families of the deceased."

Later, Dr. Ogle held her own press conference and let the media know just how daunting a task it was going to be for her and Licking County Coroner Robert Raker. Ogle said, "This is a very complicated and unusual case, but we are using our standard procedures. It can be a very lengthy process. There are numerous rigorous forensic procedures involved. In order to preserve evidence, the bodies were immediately transported from the tree to the Licking County Coroner's Office." Because of the difficult task concering bodies that had been cut up after death by Matthew Hoffman, the unusual aspect of two coroners offices becoming inovled had taken place. This was not a normal procedure, but then there was nothing normal about these murders as compared to most.

Dr. Ogle added that before the autopsies began, she met with the victims' family members to answer their questions and offer support to them. Ogle said, "My priority was the family. I wanted to make sure I'd taken good care of explaining things to them before I spoke about the victims to other people. People react differently

to grief, each experiencing loss in their own way, and as
death investigations proceed, the bereaved require different answers as they process their loss. Some people need
all the forensic details in order to get closure. Some people can move on without all the details."

Ogle added that she hoped the autopsies would help
in the prosecution of the case. "We're not in a hurry at
this point. It's critical to get every detail right in coming
up with a cause of death and to be able to provide family
and loved ones with the answers they need."

Asked by a reporter how the case had affected her, she
answered, "It would be impossible not to be emotional
about this. We're all emotional about this, but we approach it in a scientific way, not allowing our emotions
to get in front of us.

"Our entire community has been wounded in this
tragedy, and words can't describe the sorrow felt by all.
Knox County is one of the warmest, kindest and most
beautiful communities I've ever witnessed. I firmly believe that no one person can ever take that away from us.
The story of Sarah Maynard's rescue will forever be remembered as an example of extraordinary detective work
and bravery."

A follow-up question asked if this particular case had
affected her differently from past cases. Without hesitat-
ing, she said, "Yes."

Farther away, Larry, Sarah and the rest of the Maynard
family huddled inside their home, determined not to

speak with the media clamoring outside their door. To Larry it felt as if all of the planets had fallen on his head. He was dazed to the point of inertia. He couldn't eat. He could barely sleep, only dozing off on the couch once in a while. Even though it seemed like the walls of his house were closing in on him, he couldn't stand the thought of going outside and facing the media onslaught. The last thing he wanted at that point was to be besieged by questions. It was his wife, Tracy, who had to answer the phone. Soon she even stopped doing that. Most of the calls were from news agencies badgering them for information.

A neighbor was sent out on runs to bring in food for the family. All she would say to reporters was that when she saw Sarah, the girl looked physically well.

In fact, Sarah was showing a remarkable resilience. One of Larry Maynard's neighbors told a reporter, "When Sarah first arrived at her dad's house, she smiled and waved. It brought tears to my eyes. My daughter has played with Sarah on past visits."

And another neighbor said, "When Sarah's ready to face the world again, she'll have friends."

At that time, however, Larry had a sign placed on his front door that stated, "We are not ready to talk at this time."

Greg Borders, who had also said very little to reporters, met with one after the news broke about the recovery of the bodies. He said, "When the police let me back into that house for the first time, I was numb. Once it hit me, I had to get out of the house. I'll never go back to that house!"

Greg's uncle told a reporter, "Tina was very compassionate and caring. She would give you the shirt off her back. Those kids came before anyone else."

In the Apple Valley area, Stephanie Sprang's uncle, Chris Thompson, thanked the volunteer searchers for all their efforts and said, "We're going to need time to deal with this." And friends of Stephanie spoke once again about how close Tina and Stephanie had been. They said the two were nearly inseparable, and that they were both hardworking mothers who'd loved their children.

Grief and shock now ran rampant throughout the area. On the Facebook page dedicated to the victims, were one posting after another by individuals who'd known them, and many more by people who had never met them. One posting stated, "My heart is broken. God put your loving arms of comfort around Sarah and all those in mourning."

A makeshift memorial to the victims had sprung up around a large tree near the house on King Beach Road. Friends and people who didn't even know the victims brought stuffed animals, flowers and other mementos. They also brought purple ribbons to remember Tina, Stephanie, Kody and Sarah. In fact, by now the tree was festooned with numerous purple ribbons blowing in the breeze. There were dozens of balloons, flowers, candles and baseballs. Someone had written on one baseball, "We love you Kody!"

A man named Mike Page, who had dated Stephanie Sprang seven years before, showed up with an armload of purple ribbons. He told a reporter, "Stephanie is going to be sadly missed. I don't think for anyone it's sunk in yet."

And at the Dairy Queen where Tina had worked, the sign that had been there all week was altered. Instead of "Pray for our missing families," the word "missing" was now removed so that it stated, "Pray for our families." The Dairy Queen also donated a dollar from every Blizzard sold to a fund to help Sarah and Stephanie Sprang's children. The store sold 2,532 Blizzards in a very short period of time.

As the sun went down on the cold evening of November 19 members of Stephanie's and Tina's extended families gathered at Apple Lake for a memorial service and vigil. Many friends and volunteers were there as well. They lit small tea-light candles encased in cupcake holders like small boats. These candles were then set adrift on the waters of the lake. They glowed in the dark with tiny bright points of light.

The Reverend Lee Cubie of the Howard United Methodist Church addressed the crowd. "We're here tonight to show that we can raise a light in this world that is greater than any darkness or gloom that may overcome us."

Julie Arthur was there with her sixteen-year-old daughter, Paige, and said, "This is Knox County. We support each other. It doesn't matter if you knew them. They were mothers. They were children."

* * *

On Friday, November 19, 2010, Chief Forensic Patholo-
gist C. Jeff Lee, who was working with Jennifer Ogle and
Robert Raker on the case, began the autopsy process.
The task was formidable, given the state of the body
parts. Lee noted that besides the remains in the official
body bags, there were "several black plastic trash bags
containing portions of three dismembered bodies inter-
mingled with clothing, towels and personal possessions."
It was even difficult to differentiate which clothing had
been worn by Tina Herrmann and which by Stephanie
Sprang.

After that was sorted out, Lee noted that the upper
part of a gray hooded sweatshirt that had belonged to
Tina revealed three cuts, as did the upper portion of her
back. The upper right portion of the front of Tina's
T-shirt also showed a three-inch cut and a one-inch cut.

Lee stated, "The well-developed, adult female body
[Tina] is disarticulated at the neck, across the upper abdomen, bilateral shoulder joints, bilateral hip joints and
bilateral knee joints." A plain gold ring was present on
the second finger of the right hand, and there was no
polish on the nails.

Several postmortem wounds were identified, including two abrasions near the right eye and jagged wounds
on the posterior scalp and back of the neck. There were
a few incised wounds near the left shoulder. But what
really stood out was a fourteen-inch vertically oriented
incised wound running from the upper portion of the

chest to the lower part of the torso. This was most likely the fatal wound. There were smaller incised wounds lower on the torso, and wounds on the hands and fingers, as well as some wounds on the left thigh. Actual deep stab wounds were catalogued later in the report.

Tina's heart was determined to be of a normal size and shape, but there was an incised wound to the aorta. The lungs had suffered stab wounds as well, with three stab wounds to the upper right lung, and two in its lower portions. There were three stab wounds to the left lung. There were no fractures to the skull, though there was a hemorrhage near the parietal bones.

Stephanie's autopsy was much the same as Tina's had been. She too had suffered from several deep knife wounds, as well as additional nonfatal wounds. She also had abrasions and perimortem bruises on her body. Not unlike Tina, Stephanie's body had been dismembered at the joints and showed a certain amount of sophistication in the cutting technique.

Kody's autopsy revealed seven deep stab wounds to the torso, including one on the right upper chest, described as a "gaping stab wound passing downward, backward and to the left through the subcutaneous tissue." There was a similar wound to the left lung. The left part of his abdomen had sustained a stab wound one inch in depth. And there were four stab wounds to the back, all of them about one and a half inches deep. Lee also noted that there appeared to be blunt force trauma to the head, and as with the other bodies, "postmortem dismemberment with an attempt at concealment."

From the victims' bodies, it was evident that Matthew Hoffman knew how to kill someone with a knife. In all three cases, the cause of death was stabbing, not blunt force trauma or other means.

Gary Ludwig, a supervisor with the wildlife division of the Ohio Department of Natural Resources, said that the tree in which the bodies had been found was being cut down to keep it from "becoming a sightseeing thing." The last thing the department wanted was curious people tromping out to the site where Hoffman had disposed of his victims' bodies.

Even after the recovery of the bodies, some people were skeptical that Matthew Hoffman had committed the crimes by himself. A man named Joe S contacted Detective Sergeant Roger Brown and said that he'd worked with Hoffman a month previously. Joe discounted other descriptions of Hoffman as a total loner and related, "Matt and [a] friend drove to Charles Mill to get paid for a job. They were paid by check. The store cashed their checks for them. I am just curious as to who his friend was. He was a big husky guy. They were driving a Chevy S-10, and the bed was wooden, I believe." Joe also said he recalled the husky guy talking about having been in Colorado.

Joe went on to say that he didn't think Hoffman seemed very strong; according to him, Hoffman looked more like a junkie. Joe was certain that the husky man had helped Hoffman in all the crimes.

Most other opinions, however, especially in law enforcement, agreed that Matthew Hoffman had been the sole killer of Tina, Kody and Stephanie. They knew he had a penchant for breaking into people's residences, as his Colorado crime had shown.

And they also knew that Hoffman had plenty of upper-body strength and that he worked out. There was even an unexpected connection between Hoffman and Stephanie Sprang in that regard: police learned from Steve Mullins, owner of Body Basics gym in Mount Vernon, that Matthew Hoffman had been a member there and Stephanie Sprang had been on the cleaning crew. Mullins noted that Hoffman would generally come in shortly before closing time, and Stephanie and the cleaning crew would come in after hours when the gym was already closed. Mullins didn't know whether the two had ever crossed paths, but the information renewed speculation that Matthew Hoffman might have met, or at least seen, Stephanie before the crimes were committed on November 10.

TWENTY-SEVEN

Matt Hoffman's Statement

The formal written confession by Matthew Hoffman came on Saturday, November 20, 2010. Detective David Light said, "Hoffman's attorneys typed his confession and he signed it as well as making several corrections." Matthew Hoffman had to write a statement about what he had done in connection with Tina, Sarah, Kody and Stephanie. When it was finished, the authorities believed it was a combination of the truth, half truths and downright lies.

Hoffman began by saying that he had parked his car in Howard (Apple Valley) and walked to the area of Tina's residence. He then went into a patch of woods across the street shortly after midnight on November 10. He had a sleeping bag with him and slept in it during the nighttime hours.

Hoffman related that there were two vehicles parked near the house, and he said he woke up when one of them, the gray car (probably Greg Borders's), left during the early morning hours. Hoffman said that he then went back to sleep until around nine in the morning. He added that he stayed in the woods until the woman of the residence left in the pickup truck.

Since there were no more vehicles at the house, Hoffman walked across the street and tried entering the front door, but it was locked. He then went to the garage door and found it was not closed all the way. He slid under the door and entered the garage, then kicked in the door from the garage to the interior of the house. By that time it was around 10:30 AM as far as he could tell. The investigators believed this was probably true, since Tina Herrmann was known to be out of the house at that point.

Hoffman's statement continued, "I looked around the house to make sure that no one else was there. Even if I did not take anything, there was a certain amount of excitement in being in someone else's home without them being there."

Hoffman wrote that he was looking for anything of value that he could easily carry out of the house, items like jewelry and money. He searched around the house for about an hour and stated that he didn't "find anything of real value."

Hoffman said he was getting ready to leave when he heard a vehicle pull up in the driveway. If this is correct, he stayed in the house almost two hours before anyone came home, which is unusual in a burglary. Hoffman said he was in a back bedroom and couldn't exit the house without breaking a window and jumping out. He added, "I brought my knife for a certain amount of intimidation in case I ran into someone and needed to make an escape."

When Tina Herrmann made her way to the back bedroom, Hoffman confronted her and made her lie down on the bed, facedown. He said he had a blackjack and was going to try and knock her out. He hit her in the back of the head a couple of times, but it did not knock her out; he claimed that then he started panicking and before he knew it, the woman's friend came into the bedroom. This second woman yelled at him and his sense of panic increased.

Hoffman grabbed his knife, which he said he'd put down on the nightstand until that moment, and stabbed the woman on the bed (Tina) through her back twice. Then he chased down the other woman (Stephanie Sprang), who had run into Sarah's room, and stabbed her a couple of times in the chest. Hoffman believed this was a girl's bedroom, based on the room's contents. In many ways, Hoffman's claim that Stephanie ran to Sarah's bedroom didn't make sense, since Stephanie knew that house, and knew that Sarah's bedroom would be a trap with no exit. It's quite possible he was lying about this, and had actually dragged Stephanie into that bedroom to kill her. The only reason she may have run into Sarah's bedroom was that she panicked and fled to that area of the house.

Hoffman said he made sure the woman who had

yelled at him was dead, and then returned to the bedroom where the first woman was still lying facedown. He stabbed her again and again until he was sure she was dead as well.

Hoffman claimed that by then, he was in a total state of shock. He wandered around the house "slowly coming to a realization of what I had done and how bad it was." There was a dog in the house that would not stop barking, so he killed it too. Eventually, Hoffman said, he decided to dispose of the bodies and burn the house down.

At first he considered loading the women's bodies into the Jeep parked in the garage and driving them to a Foundation Park pond. He said he planned to drive the Jeep into the pond and then swim away as the vehicle sank. But then, he wrote, he realized that the water would be very cold and he might not be able to make it to shore. Hoffman continued, "I decided to process the bodies and dispose of them inside of a tree that I knew was hollow." By "process the bodies," he meant dismember them into small sizes that he could put into trash bags.

Hoffman claimed that he dragged the women's bodies into the bathroom, where he began "processing" them. He said he used garbage bags he found in the house and placed the body parts inside of them. Once he had finished cutting up the bodies, he moved the Jeep into the garage from the driveway where it had been parked, to load up the body bags. From the time he killed Tina and Stephanie until the kids got home from school, was at least an hour and a half. He still had a couple of bags left to load when he heard children come into the house. He knew there was a small amount of blood on the floor at the front door due to his having placed a bag there before he decided how best to load all the bags into the Jeep.

Hoffman said he was in the hallway when the children first came into the house, and quickly decided he had to do something. He ran to the front door, and the girl slipped past him and ran into a bedroom. Hoffman related, "I immediately stabbed the boy in the chest a couple of times." That would indicate that Kody hadn't turned around toward the door before he was killed. Sarah thought that he had turned and was making his way toward the door. Evidence, seemed to prove that Sarah was correct. The fatal stab wound to Kody was in the back of his head and there was another stab wound to his back.

Hoffman then ran to the bedroom where the girl had gone to make sure she wasn't calling for help and added, "I saw the girl was not on the phone and I could not bring myself to kill her." This was in direct contradiction to Sarah, who said that she was on the phone but he grabbed her before she could use it.

Hoffman wrote that the girl said she thought he was going to kill her, but he told her he wouldn't and "everything was fine." She was suspicious about blood in her bedroom, but Hoffman had already dumped motor oil on those blood spots to try and change their appearance. Or that was at least his version now. He told her they were not blood spots but rather something else. Sarah did not believe him about the blood. Then he said he lied and told her that he had "tasered" her brother, who was still alive. Sarah did not believe him about this, and in fact, he may have not mentioned this tasering at all to her during the actual events of November 10th. More likely he was just inserting this now, since Sarah did not mention the taser comment at all.

Hoffman's statement continued with him saying that he had already found duct tape in the house and so he used that to bind Sarah's hands together and put a pillowcase over her head. Sarah did not say where the duct tape came from, and other individuals commented that Hoffman often had duct tape in his car.

Then he said he led her to the garage where he looked for rope to tie her up more securely. Sarah denied this and related that he took her to the basement, cut off some rope from a sled and tied her up with that. Hoffman agreed that he did find some rope and used this to bind her hands and feet. After that was done, he carried her back to the kitchen and laid her on the floor. Sarah said that it was at that point that the pillowcase that he had placed over her head fell off.

He claimed, "I did not want to harm the little girl, and I do not believe she saw anything. At some point in time I learned her name was Sarah from a baseball card on the fridge."

After Sarah was laid on the kitchen floor, Hoffman said he "processed" the boy. The boy was taken to the same bathroom where Hoffman had dismembered the bodies of the two women. After he was done with the boy, Hoffman took all the bags to the Jeep and placed them on the backseat. He then gathered up a pile of blankets and placed them in the car as well. Finally he picked up Sarah from the kitchen and put her in the backseat of the Jeep under the blankets and next to the trash bags filled with body parts.

Hoffman said he drove to the baseball field on Pipesville Road, parked the Jeep there with Sarah inside, locked the car and walked back to where his own car was. He then drove his car back to the ball field and waited until dark to transfer Sarah from the Jeep into his car.

Matt said that he drove Sarah to his house on Columbus Road, where he claimed, "I felt that she [Sarah] was still sufficiently subdued, and I drove to McDonald's. I brought back food, removed her bonds and we ate. I tried to comfort her and told her everything would be fine." Sarah adamantly denied all of this story later, insisting that he hadn't left her alone, hadn't removed her bindings, that the only food he'd given her—the cereal with the sour milk—had been after she'd had to beg for something to eat, nor had he comforted her in any way.

In Hoffman's version of events, he said that after they ate, he tied Sarah back up and claimed, "I made her a bed out of leaves, covered it with blankets and placed her on the bed." He also boasted, "She liked that bed, it was extremely comfy." Sarah's account differed here; she said that at this point she had been left not on the bed of leaves but on the floor of a cold dark bathroom.

By now it was 9:00 or 10:00 PM on Thursday, November 10, and Hoffman said he was so exhausted he fell asleep for a couple of hours. He set his alarm clock for midnight and then drove his car up to the hunting preserve where he knew about the hollow tree. He said he drove there with his climbing gear first to scout out the area, and so that if he was pulled over, there wouldn't be bags of body parts found inside his vehicle.

Hoffman dropped off his climbing gear at the hollow tree, then he drove the Toyota to Walmart in Mount Vernon where he purchased the large garbage bags and two tarps. He explained that he'd wanted heavier garbage bags because he said there were too many small bags in the Jeep and they were not very strong.

After these purchases, Hoffman said he drove to a parking lot near the river, then walked to where he'd left the Jeep at the ballpark and drove it to the hunting preserve and the hollow tree. By then it was around 2:30 AM, November 11. It took him awhile to get all the body bags inside the hollow of the tree, so it was almost daylight by the time he finished. Then he drove the Jeep back to Tina's residence and parked it in the garage. He located gas cans in the garage and loaded them into Tina's pickup truck.

Hoffman drove off in the pickup truck with plans to buy gasoline, return to the house and set the whole place on fire. However, he said, the pickup truck was not acting right and would not stay in gear. Deciding the trip was taking too long, Hoffman abandoned the pickup truck at a parking lot near Kenyon College and walked back to his Toyota Yaris on the Gap Trail. It was a greater distance than he supposed, and he did not reach his car until sometime between 9:00 and 10:00 AM.

Hoffman then drove back to his residence on Columbus Road and, as he put it, "took care of Sarah." He said she had wet herself and that she did so every time she fell asleep. Hoffman said he let her shower and get into some of his clothes. He said he apologized to her for all of this and then made her breakfast. Sarah denied he ever let her shower and said he certainly didn't make her breakfast, other than the bowl of cereal with sour milk.

Hoffman stated that she asked him a lot of questions at this time and he kept telling her everything was fine. He also said he was extremely tired from all his exertions. Hoffman stated that he set up some movies on a DVD player and they watched *Iron Man* and *Iron Man 2* (something Sarah also refuted). He added he wanted to sleep but was afraid to do so, fearing that Sarah might escape. Then he added a line that Sarah would adamantly deny: "I slept a little with my arms around her, and did this [to] ensure she would not leave, while at the same time, not having to tie her up."

Hoffman wrote that he then did her laundry, because she wanted to wear her own clothes. He said he had to do this a lot, because every time she fell asleep she would wet her clothes. He would let her shower every time this happened, he claimed, and that he made her bed of leaves very comfortable. He also claimed, "She really did like to be in that bed." Once again, Sarah denied all of this.

At around 6:30 PM on November 11, Hoffman drove

back to where he had left Tina's pickup truck, intending to collect the gas cans from the truck and finish his plan to burn down Tina's residence. But then a deputy came walking over to his vehicle, demanding to know who he was and why he was there. Hoffman handed over his driver's license and told the deputy that he was waiting for his girlfriend, Sarah, to get off work. The deputy let him go, but not before Hoffman became suspicious that law enforcement already knew about the crimes at the house on King Beach Drive.

Hoffman said at that point he knew he could not go and burn the house down as planned, so instead he drove back to his own residence where he built a campfire in the backyard, drank a bottle of wine and burned his shoes. He said he then slept for a couple of hours and woke around midnight. After that he went down to the basement and said that he let Sarah use the bathroom. He related that he hoped this would prevent her from having any more "accidents."

At this point, Hoffman wrote, he decided he had to go back to the woods near the house on King Beach Drive where he'd left his backpack and sleeping bag, before they were discovered. He drove to a parking lot at Millwood and then rode his bike to the hill behind the spillway of Apple Valley Lake. From there he slowly made his way on foot to the woods to retrieve the pocketknife and ball cap from his backpack and sleeping bag. He wrote nothing of the other things he left behind. By then it was almost daylight on the morning of Friday, November 12. He also saw a lot of police activity at the house on King

Beach Drive. Apparently he was not spotted, and Hoffman made his way back to his bike, and then to his car in Millwood. He thought the time by then was 9:00 AM.

Hoffman again related things that Sarah would adamantly deny, for example claiming that when he returned home, he made breakfast for the two of them and had her do the dishes. He then said the word "ransom" to her and had her look it up in the dictionary. Hoffman added that he would be keeping her for a while, and declared that he had accomplices in all of this and they were already in negotiations with her family.

He said that he did not want to gag her, so she might hear his accomplices at times outside the house. By contrast, Sarah said she was gagged whenever he left the house. Hoffman related, "I told her all those things so that if she heard voices outside the house, she would not scream for help. I told her that she would not be harmed in any way if she complied with everything. I told her she would most likely be home by Christmas."

That same day, Hoffman said he put Sarah in a closet that he could lock from the outside. He wrote that she could read *Treasure Island* or get some sleep in there. By this means, he said he was able to sleep for a few hours on Friday afternoon. Sarah denied that she'd been given anything to read.

Eventually he woke up and, he wrote, he once again let Sarah shower, and on Friday night they had hamburgers for dinner (Sarah said this, too, did not happen). Hoffman added that she wanted to go to bed early, so he let her get back into her clothes since she had been wearing some of his clothing. Again he related that he tied her back up and she went to sleep on the bed of leaves in the basement.

Hoffman declared that Friday night was the first night he was able to get a good night's rest. Once again he claimed that when he got up, he let Sarah shower and he did laundry. Then he wrote that after her shower they talked and he let her play Wii. Sarah said none of that ever happened.

He also related that he showed Sarah sexual videos on the computer and that they had consensual oral sex, all of which Sarah adamantly denied. After that, Hoffman wrote, they just hung out together.

All of Hoffman's statement up to this point had been typed, but Hoffman later added a handwritten line alleging that this was the day Sarah first complained about the problem of wetting herself. Hoffman said he was going to get her some pull-up diapers the next day, but for the time being he just made her some out of plastic trash bags.

Later that night, he tied her once again on her bed of leaves in the basement and went to sleep as well. Then in a terse addition, he added, "The police came on Sunday morning, and I was glad that she was able to leave to be reunited with her family. I would not have hurt her. I could not hurt her."

Hoffman claimed his intention all along had been to give Sarah more and more freedom until she could eventually run away. Then, Hoffman said, he planned to go on the run himself. He declared that he had not planned far enough in advance as to where he would run.

Hoffman swore in writing that he had not entered the house on King Beach Drive planning to kill anyone. "I did not know a single one of them. I did not know their names and I did not know who all lived at that house." This was, of course, counter to statements by others that Stephanie Sprang did know Matthew Hoffman and she may have even done work at his residence. There were some people who believed that he might have met Tina before.

Hoffman wrote that he'd picked that particular house because there were no nearby neighbors, and because he had also noticed before the events of November 10 that the garage door to the house was ajar. He asserted that "I did not want to kill anyone, and I tried to just knock the first woman out so that I would be able to escape. This was not working, a second woman showed up, and things quickly spiraled out of control. They kept escalating and I was panicking. I only chose to process the bodies to make their disposal easier."

TWENTY-EIGHT

Questions

The authorities did not believe much of what Matthew Hoffman had told his attorneys to write in the statement, and had numerous questions to which he had to give written answers. Detective David Light noted, "Investigators were able to review the confession and submit questions. After Hoffman answered the questions, his attorneys wrote his answers and he initialed the answers and signed each page."

The questions were as follows:

1. "Where exactly are the sleeping bag/backpack hidden in the field across from the house?" Hoffman wrote, "See photo." Apparently he had marked on a photo of the woods where they could be located.

2. "You said you went to look for money, jewelry, yet you left jewelry in a purse at the house. Explain." Hoffman's reply was, "As the result of being discovered, and the ensuing deaths, jewelry was no longer an issue."

3. "Where were you in the house when you first heard Tina in the driveway? Did she enter the house through garage or front door? Why were you unable to exit through the back door when you first heard her in the driveway?" Hoffman: "I didn't hear her enter. Assume front door."

4. "What was said between you and Tina during the initial confrontation?" Hoffman: "No conversation. I brandished knife to intimidate her."

5. "Why not tie Tina up to make your escape instead of knocking her out?" Hoffman: "If I had time, I would have. Was interrupted by second woman."

6. "Did you strike woman #2 [Stephanie] or the boy [Kody] with the blackjack?" Hoffman: "No."

7. "How could you tell both women were dead?" Hoffman: "It was evident."

8. "Where was the dog when you killed it?" Hoffman: "Bathtub."

9. "How did you know how to 'process' the bodies using only a knife? How did you cut around bone joints,

etc?" Hoffman: "It's general knowledge that you can't cut through bone with a knife."

10. "When you opened the garage door, did you use the automatic opener or do it by hand?" Hoffman: "Never used the opener."

11. "Where did you find the Jeep keys?" Hoffman: "They were in the ignition."

12. "You saw evidence of children in the house, why did you not get out of there before the end of school time when they would have been expected home?" Hoffman: "Assumed school went later than it did."

13. "What happened to the pillowcase you put over Sarah's head? Where did you last leave it?" Hoffman: "Fell off in transit from garage to kitchen." [Sarah said it fell off from the basement to the kitchen].

14. "Where did you find rope in the basement?" Here Hoffman crossed out "basement" and wrote "garage" in its place. The rest of the answer was "from a sled." [Sarah said it was from the basement].

15. "How did you learn Sarah's name including her middle name, when you first asked if she was Sarah Marie Maynard?" Hoffman: "Never asked if she was SMM." Sarah didn't know if this was true or not. She was uncertain if he may have seen her someplace in the area before November 10th.

16. "How did you get Sarah into your house? Where did you park the Yaris when you did this?" Answer for the first part: "Carried her." For the second part: "My backyard."

17. "Says you set the alarm for midnight Wednesday, got up and drove to wildlife area to drop gear and check it out. Then went to Wal-Mart on return. But you were at Wal-Mart at midnight (12:08 AM). Is this correct? Is the time off?" Hoffman: "Believe chronology of events accurate. Could Wal-Mart clocks be off?"

18. "The video at Wal-Mart showed your car arriving from the east and leaving toward the east. What route did you take from the tree to Wal-Mart? Explain this?" Hoffman: "Skirted city to avoid traffic."

19. "How many of the newly purchased Wal-Mart large garbage bags did you use? Why did you leave them in the garage if the bags with the bodies were already in the Jeep at the ball field?" Hoffman: "They were left there when I returned the Jeep."

20. "Why did you buy the orange and black Halloween shirt at Wal-Mart?" Hoffman: "Because it was only one dollar. It was right by the only open checkout counter. It was an impulse purchase."

21. "What did you do with the clothing you were wearing? Did you clean or destroy any of it?" Hoffman circled the word "clean," and wrote, "Washed them."

22. "There was no evidence of burnt shoes in the fire remnants in the backyard. Where did you put them

after you burned them? Two pairs of shoes, athletic
and boots, were found in house matching prints at
the scene. Did you put them through the washing
machine? Do you have more than one pair of the
same shoes?" Hoffman: "Burned in back yard. Did
not move ashes. Yes, only pair worn at AV [Apple Val-
ley] house were shoes that I burned. Matching shoes
were identical to burned shoes, purchased several
months after initial purchase."

23. "Why was it so important to retrieve pocket knife
    and ball cap?" Hoffman: "Incriminating evidence."
    This did not make a whole lot of sense, since he left
    so much other incriminating evidence behind there.
    Why the baseball cap and pocket knife were more
    incriminating in his mind than the other items, he
    did not say.

24. "Did you watch the house when you went back to the
    backpack, sleeping bag? What did you see?" Hoffman:
    "Yes. Deputies stationed at both ends of King Beach
    Drive house. Illuminated by spotlights and police
    emergency lights."

Questions 25 to 28 dealt with the specifics of the sexual assault on Sarah, a minor. Hoffman's replies corrobo-
rated what Sarah said he had done. She adamantly denied,
however, that anything he and she did was consensual.
She noted that it was all under duress and she complied
because she was afraid he would kill her if she didn't.

29. "After you returned to your house on Friday morning, did you ever leave again before police arrived on Sunday?" Hoffman: "Yes. Retrieved climbing gear. Had been left away from tree, but still in wildlife area. After retrieving gear went straight home. Had groceries in house."

30. "Did you ever join a search party or show up at a meeting of searchers during the event?" Hoffman: "No."

31. "What were you doing for money before and during the last weeks?" Hoffman: "Unemployment compensation."

32. "Did you see the children leave for school? Get on the bus?" Hoffman: "No."

33. "Did you wipe down the truck for prints, evidence?" Hoffman: "No, wore gloves."

34. "Where did you put the blankets you had wrapped Sarah with in the Jeep?" Hoffman: "Used for bed at Columbus Road."

35. "How many pair of gloves did you take into the house? Did you use other gloves from the house or from other sources over the course of the event?" Hoffman answered that he took only one pair of gloves into the King Beach Drive residence, and that he used two pairs of gloves during the whole four-day episode. This was counter to the evidence that two pairs of gloves were used in the house.

After the questions were answered, Detective David Light and Special Agent Joe Dietz signed the bottom of the agreement between Hoffman and his attorneys and Prosecutor John Thatcher.

That same day Detective Doug Turpen and Lieutenant Gary Rohler received information from Matthew Hoffman via his attorneys indicating where he had left clothing and other items in the woods across the street from the King Beach Drive address. The officers went there and found two empty water bottles, a backpack and a camouflage jacket stuffed under some weeds.

Quite a few additional items were seized from the woods. These included a gray pullover top, camouflage sweatpants, a pair of boot socks and a green headlamp. A blue lighter and matches were found, as well as a tube of camouflage makeup, one apple and assorted candy and peanut wrappers. Why Hoffman left these items and came back only for the ball cap and pocketknife remained a mystery.

As mentioned earlier, many people did not believe the particulars of Matt Hoffman's statement or his answers to the investigators' follow-up questions, considering Hoffman's recollections to be a combination of half truths and outright lies. Larry Maynard was definitely in that group. He did not believe Hoffman's claim that he had picked Tina's residence at random. Larry speculated that perhaps Hoffman knew or had previously met Tina or Stephanie, or maybe he'd seen Sarah at the house. Whatever the reason, Larry firmly believed that Hoffman had purposefully targeted the house, and not just to rob it.

"What kind of burglar spends all that time in a house, not knowing when a person will come back home?" Larry questioned. A thief, he reasoned, would "want to get in and out of there as soon as possible. And with many valuable items in the house, why didn't he take them after he had killed Tina and Stephanie? He had plenty of time to leave before Sarah and Kody got home. His first action should have been to get out of the house as soon as possible. From just looking around the house, he had to know that a boy and girl lived there." Larry was particularly disturbed that Hoffman had left Tina's purse behind. "I could never figure out why Hoffman left Tina's purse in the garage. It contained two rings and the gold necklace with the dolphin on it. These were expensive items. If he had been there to rob the place, then that should have been the first things he carried out with him when he went with Sarah in Stephanie's Jeep to the baseball-field parking lot. Why leave that purse in the garage? That's where the detectives found it.

"In my heart I don't believe Matthew Hoffman went there to just rob the place. I mean, why did he stay around all that time before Tina ever got home? And then he spent all the extra time in the house until the kids got home from school? He knew how much more risky that made his situation. He said he'd seen Greg drive off in his vehicle that morning. How did he know that Greg wasn't coming home [later]?" Larry felt the entire scenario had been preplanned. "I believe he was just marking time until the kids got home so that he could kill Kody and snatch Sarah. He even said that he saw her photo on the refrigerator in the house. So he knew she lived there, and wasn't surprised at all when they came home from school.

"And I don't believe anything he said about treating Sarah well when he had her at his house. He claimed he let her shower, fed her well and watched DVD movies with her. Sarah told me none of those things happened. He just wrote all that stuff to make himself look better. I believe that most of the stuff he said, other than his timeline of moving vehicles and things like that, was all a lie. He just wanted to make people think things had spun out of control. I believe that as soon as he stepped foot inside that house, he planned to kill. Otherwise, why bring the blackjack and the knife? He said it was just to threaten, but he was big enough to threaten Tina, Stephanie, Kody or Sarah without a knife."

Ultimately, Larry said, "There were a lot of other items in that house that Hoffman didn't take. Why not, if it was just a burglary? None of that made any sense. He had to have other reasons for going in there and doing what he did. More than anything else, those reasons drive me crazy thinking about them. I can't believe it was just a random act—that he picked that house out of all the houses in the area. There had to be a reason—but I don't know what it is. And very little of what he said in his confession can be taken as the truth."

TWENTY-NINE

Thoughts and Prayers

The first Sunday after the news broke about the discovery of Tina's, Kody's and Stephanie's bodies was like no other in living memory in Mount Vernon. All the local churches addressed the news in one manner or another.

At the Trinity Worship Center, which Sarah Maynard had attended with a friend only weeks before the crimes, Reverend Donald Matolyak told a reporter before the service, "What do you say to people, in the midst of what's perhaps the most terrible evil that's been perpetrated in this community? I want to present a picture of hope."

During his address to the congregation, Reverend Matolyak declared that Matthew Hoffman was just one person, and they did not have to live in fear. He pointed out how the community had embraced the victims while they were still "missing" and volunteered in droves to find them. "Into the darkness we shine. Out of the ashes we rise." Matolyak even asked the congregation to pray for the "forgotten victims"—Matthew Hoffman's family members—reminding people that they were not part of what Hoffman had done.

Brenda Renshaw, who was a member of the church and knew Sarah, related, "For young people, we want them to believe that God loves all of us, even if that's hard to believe at a time like this. It's going to take a long while, but it's going to get back to where we feel normal like before."

Late on Monday, November 22, a fire was reported on the deck of the house on King Beach Drive where Tina, Kody and Stephanie had been killed. A fire crew was sent and they easily put out the fire, but just who was responsible for starting it or why it had been set was not apparent. Some people in the community thought that it was a message to Greg Borders not to move back into the house. Others thought that someone wanted the house to burn down to erase the memory of what had happened there.

The next day, November 23, an investigation into the fire was begun. On that same day, Matthew Hoffman and his attorneys waived the scheduled court hearing. And the families of Tina Herrmann, Kody Maynard and Stephanie Sprang were receiving friends and family at public visitations, with private funerals to follow the next day.

* * *

That Tuesday at Flowers-Snyder Funeral Home up in
Mount Vernon, people were saying good-bye to Stephanie Sprang. Stephanie's mother, Pat Cullins, had written
a statement to the community at large. It read, "I want
to thank everyone who has been supporting our family
at this time of crisis. It makes you realize how many caring people there are in such a wicked world. It makes me
proud to say I live in Mount Vernon because the community support has amazed me.

"I wish I could thank everyone personally, but I just
know I am talking to each one of you when I express my
deepest thanks to each of you. I know that Stephanie
thanks you all. I want to also thank the Sheriff, FBI and
all Law Enforcement who worked long and hard to find
my daughter, at times with little sleep. You have my sin-
cere thanks."

Cars were parked for blocks around the funeral home.
Inside, a photo montage documenting Stephanie's forty-
one-year life was projected on a screen, the photos fading
in and out. There were photos of Stephanie as a young
girl—as a toddler in a winter coat, a little girl in a frilly
dress, a teenager nearing high school graduation—and
later photos, depicting her in a long white wedding
gown, or with family members around a Christmas tree.
There was also a large memorial photo of Stephanie, with
her portrait on the right side of the frame, and a light-
house on an oceanside cliff on the left. Below it were the
words, "In Loving Memory Stephanie L. Sprang. Born

on Saturday, November 1, 1969. Died on Wednesday, November 10, 2010."

A poem titled "Tomorrow" was printed on handouts distributed during the visiting hours. The poem expressed that when a person woke up in the mornings and began crying, Stephanie wished that the person wouldn't do so. She wanted to let the person know that she knew they loved her, and she loved them as well. She also wanted them to know that whenever that person thought of her, she wasn't far away at all, but right there in their heart.

Sheriff David Barber paid his respects and attended the memorial service, as did many friends and members of the community, including Randall Alcie, who knew Stephanie from frequent karaoke nights. Randall told a reporter that Stephanie was a good singer who especially liked rock and party songs, and that "she was always smiling. Always having a good time. I never saw her down. She was a character, a real character. Full of life and enjoyed living."

Another person who attended the memorial said, "She was a beautiful person inside and out. It's unreal that somebody could do something like this to her, to a family. A whole community is hurting and pulling together."

Other friends showed up from the golf course where Stephanie had once worked. Shannon Beheler, who had been one of Stephanie's golfing partners, said, "Her laugh was unmistakable. Just loud and always full of joy. You always knew what hole she was on because you could hear that laugh."

* * *

Also on Tuesday, November 23, 2010, public visiting hours were held for Tina Herrmann and Kody Maynard at the Peace Lutheran Church in Gahanna, about forty miles from Apple Valley. Lines of mourners entered the sanctuary. Incredibly, Sarah Maynard was there, surrounded by family, greeting one person after another, including Sheriff David Barber. As the *Mount Vernon News* noted, "No child should have to say goodbye to her mother and her brother in the same day. But that's what Sarah did, just nine days after she was freed and brought home to other family members."

A longtime friend related later about the Herrmann and Maynard families, "They're surrounded by family and they're doing the best that they can. I'm sure tomorrow at the funeral it's going to be a lot worse, but they're keeping their heads up."

Larry recalled, "I was in a daze most of the time. It didn't seem real. It was like this was all a bad dream and I'd wake up at some later time. All I could think about was Kody and Tina."

In a written statement at the memorial, Larry expressed, "We wish to take a moment to thank the nation for the outpouring of love, prayers and support that you all continue to provide. To the residents of Knox County who grieve with us as well, we would like to share that all of you who were touched by this tragedy, whether directly or indirectly, are in our hearts and prayers."

There was also soon a statement to the media: "Tina

Rose Herrmann, age 32, and Kody Alexander Maynard, age 11, were unfortunately taken away from us on Wednesday, November 10, 2010. Tina was a courageous and energetic woman whose greatest joy in life was being a mother. She worked at Dairy Queen in Mount Vernon and had the ability to connect with some of the simpler things in life, like blooming sunflowers or her dolphin collection. Her beloved son, Kody, a gentle child with an enormous heart, was a 5th grader at East Knox School. He enjoyed all sports, especially baseball.

"Tina and Kody will be missed by many loving friends and family," the statement continued, giving a long list of family members and friends and then ending with: "In lieu of flowers, contributions may be made at any Fifth Third Bank to the Sarah Maynard Benefit Fund. The Herrmann and Maynard families would like to extend a heartfelt thank-you to all those in the community who reached out in love and concern during this very difficult time."

Despite the request for no flowers, there were mounds of blooms at the visitation; the two closed caskets were surrounded by them. Friends walked out of the church with sunflowers, Tina's favorite flower, and paper baseballs inscribed with Kody's name, birth date and death date. Well-wishers could write their thoughts directly onto the baseballs.

Dee Hall, whose grandson had attended school with Kody, said, "It's part of the healing process for this community. We don't experience stuff like this every day here. I'd like to believe that something this horrific has brought the community closer together."

Valerie Haythorn, the Dairy Queen manager where Tina had worked, and who had been the first person not only to report Tina missing but also to see the interior of the house and call the police, closed the restaurant for the day so that all employees could go to Gahana for the visiting hours.

Eleven-year-old Keisha whose mother was a coworker of Tina's, told a reporter, "I wrote [on the baseball], 'We miss you, and will always miss you.'" And Keisha's mother, Teresa said, "When I pull in to work, I expect to find [Tina's] truck there. She was a joker and full of life. Sarah was being very, very strong. I couldn't imagine being that strong. She would flick rubber bands at work and sing 'Leaving on a Jet Plane.' It's like a really bad nightmare that I haven't woken up from. We don't understand why something like this happened. It just doesn't make sense."

Friends also signed an online guestbook in remembrance of Tina and Kody. One person wrote, "As the holidays approach, I will keep you Sarah, and your dad Larry in my thoughts and prayers. Just remember that your mom and brother will be with you always when you look up in the sky."

Another person wrote, "Just sending you love and support in this very difficult time. I am forever changed and want you to know that you will be in my thoughts and prayers for the rest of my life."

All around Apple Valley, purple ribbons hung from mailboxes and light posts. At the home where Tina and the kids had lived on King Beach Drive, the memorial around the tree in the front yard kept growing and growing. It contained purple balloons, white crosses, stuffed animals, candles and a wind chime. A handwritten note on the tree proclaimed, "Watch over the Maynard Family."

THIRTY

The Grand Jury

Even though Matthew Hoffman had signed a confession, the investigators were not through gathering evidence against him. He and his attorneys had waived his scheduled court hearing, but Hoffman still awaited sentencing, and both the investigators and Knox County District Attorney's Office wanted as much physical evidence as possible to support the case against him.

Another search warrant was requested for Hoffman's residence on Columbus Road, which stated the desire "to enter and search the residence and any outbuildings for certain evidence and trace evidence including shoes, blood evidence and stolen property." Judge Paul Spurgeon signed the request at 9:06 AM on November 24, 2010.

From this second search came an array of new items

seized from Hoffman's house, including a set of fifteen golf clubs and bag, a metal jewelry box, a signed baseball, an Ohio State football and a flash drive. The items also included two chain saws, a bow, a green bag containing gas can and oil can tools, a blue plastic tub and items that had been burned and melted in a backyard fire pit. The investigators believed that some items were stolen from houses other than Tina's house, and other items came from her house on King Beach Drive.

Detective Craig Feeney went with a helicopter pilot of the Ohio State Highway Patrol and took aerial photos of the scene where the three bodies had been found in the hollow tree. These area photos were taken to KCSO as part of the evidence.

The actual charges against Matthew Hoffman now comprised ten felony counts: the aggravated murders of Tina Hoffman, Stephanie Sprang and Kody Maynard ("aggravated" because the murders had occurred while engaged in a burglary); the aggravated burglary of Tina Herrmann's residence; the kidnapping and sexual assault on Sarah Maynard; tampering with evidence; and three charges concerning the abuse of corpses.

The prosecution was doing everything possible to make sure that all the charges would be factored in by a judge at sentencing. BCI&I sent a report to the Ohio Attorney General's Office detailing all of the items and DNA evidence they had collected. There were fifty items submitted by Detective David Light, ranging from the duct tape and ropes used to bind Sarah, to the blanket she had been sleeping on in Hoffman's basement. They also contained Sarah's clothing collected at the hospital, a leather sap, a SOG brand knife, and two pairs of Hoffman's boots and shoes from his residence.

Items recovered from Tina Herrmann's home included a pair of cloth gloves Hoffman had used, and numerous swabs containing blood samples as well as swatches of blood-soaked carpet.

As far as DNA evidence went, there were samples from Tina, Kody and Stephanie. There was also a sexual molestation kit pertaining to Sarah. Prosecuting Attorney John Thatcher compiled a lengthy potential witness list and submitted it to Judge Spurgeon. For KCSO, the list contained the names of Detective David Light, Sheriff David Barber, Lieutenant Gary Rohler, Detective Sergeant Roger Brown, Captain David Shaffer, Detective Tom Durbin, Detective Doug Turpen and Deputy Charles Statler. From BCI&I there were Special Agents Joe Dietz, Ed Lulla, Ed Carlini, Daniel Winterich, Gary Wilgus, Mark Kollar and George Staley. Forensic scientist Brenda Gerardi was listed, as well as FBI Special Agent Kristin Cadieux. From the Mount Vernon Police Department there were Sergeant Troy Glazier and Detective Craig Feeney. Dr. Jennifer Ogle of the Knox County Coroner's Office was listed as was Dr. Jeffrey Lee of the Licking County Coroner's Office. As far as civilians went, there was Valerie Haythorn, Tina's friend and manager at Dairy Queen, and Sarah Maynard.

For his part, Hoffman's public defender Bruce Malek felt "there is no need for a preliminary hearing in this case. Under these circumstances, we don't feel that he [Prosecutor Thatcher] has any reason to go forward with a hearing." The defense reasoning was that Hoffman had already confessed to his crimes and written out a statement.

Malek, moving in a different direction, added that Hoffman had recently been taken off a suicide watch and that "he's doing about as well as someone could be expected, who has just come off a suicide watch. He has not been released into the general population at the jail." The reason for that was the concern that some inmates would be more than happy to inflict "jailhouse justice" upon Hoffman.

Victim Assistant Director Diana Oswalt from the Knox County Prosecutor's Office was keeping in constant contact with Sarah and Larry Maynard, willing to provide counseling or simply to listen. Her office stated that the mission of the Victim Assistance Program was "to provide crime victims with information and emotional support necessary to make their way through the process of seeking justice." Oswalt said of her job, "Mostly I would just listen to victims, about their concerns. Some want to talk a lot, and others are very quiet. Either way is all right. People deal with the situation they were in, in their own way."

The other important aspect of Oswalt's job was to let Sarah and Larry know what they could expect from the upcoming case against Matthew Hoffman as it went through the judicial system; as its mission statement stated, the Victim Assistance Program sought to "ensure that the victim's rights are enforced and protected by making every effort to personally and promptly inform the victims about charges filed, hearings scheduled, the outcomes of those hearings, and dealing with the aftermath of those procedures to move forward with their lives."

Oswalt also let the Maynards know that they had a right to the reasonable return of property that was stolen, the right to communicate with the prosecutor and the right to freedom from intimidation. They also had the right to make a statement at sentencing and the right to receive information about the perpetrator after sentencing. There was even a schematic illustrating at which proceedings Sarah might be called upon to testify; these included the preliminary hearing or grand jury setting, and the actual trial. In Sarah's case, the prosecution was going the grand jury route, which would bar the news media from attending the proceedings.

On days when Sarah would not be called to testify, Oswalt could attend the proceedings and inform Sarah and Larry afterward of what had occurred; this would save the Maynards from having to appear personally in court, where they would undoubtedly be besieged by reporters. Neither Sarah nor Larry wanted to be in the limelight. As much as possible, they were trying to reconstruct normal lives, especially for Sarah.

The actual grand jury indictment of Matthew Hoffman didn't come until after the new year, on January 3, 2011. Part of the document read, "The indictment alleges that Hoffman purposely caused the deaths of Tina R Herrmann, Ms. Herrmann's son Kody Maynard, and her neighbor Stephanie Sprang on November 10, 2010. He committed the murders while he was committing the offense of Aggravated Burglary in Herrmann's residence."

Prosecutor John Thatcher said that he had called the special session of the grand jury because of the seriousness of the crimes. Grand juries in Knox County usually met only once a month, but this situation had demanded a response far beyond the routine. Thatcher added that the grand jurors listened to six hours of testimony before coming back with the indictment. In essence this grand jury hearing was Matthew Hoffman's trial pertaining to guilt, not sentencing, which would come later. The grand jurors returned a bill of indictment that found Hoffman guilty of all charges. John Thatcher wanted to make sure that all the i's were dotted and all the t's crossed in the legal proceedings.

Most family members were waiting until actual sentencing to speak to the press, though Stephanie Sprang's father, Steve Thompson, did make a short statement after the indictment, saying simply, "We don't want to say anything that might affect the outcome of the arraignment. We want to see Hoffman get everything he deserves."

THIRTY-ONE

Impact Statements

Just before formal sentencing by Judge Otho Eyster on January 5, 2011, victim impact statements were read in court. Many people were heartbroken by the brutal crimes and very angry at Matthew Hoffman, who sat at the defense table next to his attorneys as one after another, family members and friends either read their victim impact statements or had them presented to him.

One of these people was Tammy Erwin, a close friend of the Herrmann family. Tammy's husband, Terry, had grown up with the Herrmann children, Tina, Eric, Bill and Jason, and Tammy had known them for twenty-four years. Tina's mother, Barb, had babysat Tammy and Terry's children, and Tina would go along and help babysit the Erwins' kids from the time she was in elementary school until she was in high school. Tammy and Terry had helped to celebrate all the Herrmann children's high school graduations, weddings and births. They also spent Christmas and New Year's Eve with them over the years.

Before launching into the impact of the "horrific crime," Tammy thanked the SWAT team, FBI, Bureau of Missing and Exploited Children, Mount Carmel Health's Crime and Trauma Assistance Program, and everyone who had helped in the search for Tina, Kody, Sarah and Stephanie.

Tammy then said, "Kody, Tina and Stephanie were brutally murdered in Tina's home. Matthew Hoffman broke into Tina's home, robbed Sarah of her innocence and corrupted her of her morals. He lied, he cheated, he stole, he murdered and he has no respect for human or animal lives."

Tammy related that as a parent, her biggest fear was that something might happen to her children. Since the incident of November 10, she feared for her daughter to be alone at any time. When the subject was brought up at home, Tammy started crying. It had caused her many sleepless nights. Even in the daylight hours, she often would be consumed by thoughts of what had happened to Tina, Kody, Stephanie and Sarah. Tammy said it was beyond the worst horror movie she could think of.

Speaking of Sarah, Tammy said, "A sweet thirteen-year-old girl was tied up and gagged in her own home while this evil monster murdered her mother and little brother."

Tammy noted that grief, fear and insecurity would be

a part of Sarah's life to come, and said she couldn't even imagine what Sarah and her family were going through at the moment.

She said, "Matthew Hoffman is not sick, he is just evil. There is absolutely no way this beast can be rehabilitated." She likened all that Hoffman had done to a nightmare from which no one in the area would ever be fully able to wake up. She called him "the devil child of Satan" and asked that the judge show him no mercy. She also asked that he be kept in isolation in a high-security prison and never be allowed to see the light of day again. Tammy wanted Hoffman to have one bite of food a day and hoped that his cell would be filled with cobwebs and that he would soil his pants on a regular basis. She wanted Hoffman to have a tiny dark space to inhabit, as he had forced Sarah to endure.

Tammy declared that Matthew Hoffman should never have the opportunity to play ball in a prison yard. He had robbed Kody Maynard of ever playing ball again on earth. She added, however, that Kody was now playing in God's garden.

Tammy wished that there wasn't a deal in place to spare his life—that instead he would be strapped to an electric chair and executed. But since that couldn't happen, she declared, "I hope Matthew Hoffman rots in hell!"

Tina's brother Jason Herrmann also had a statement for Judge Eyster. "This horrific episode has brought immense sorrow to my family, not to mention the hundreds of friends and acquaintances." When Jason first learned of the disappearances, he said, he felt a sense of numbness and fear. He said there were days of disbelief and of hope. "It wasn't until November 17, the saddest day of my life, when my two brothers and I made the choice to walk through my sister's house, that within minutes of entering the house, we were sure we would never see our loved ones again."

Jason felt sad and angry all the time. Sad that he knew Tina had struggled in an attempt to save her children. Sad for Kody, robbed of his life at such a young age. Sadness for his niece, Sarah, who would never see her mother or brother again, and had been robbed of her innocence. Jason related that no amount of restitution or punishment would ever compensate for the struggles Sarah would face in her life. He prayed she would not constantly be haunted by what happened.

Jason said that he, and everyone around him, had had their lives turned upside down because of what Matthew Hoffman had done. His family had to face daily mental anguish and public inquiry. He and others now constantly questioned their security, their neighbors and "the good will of our common man."

"There is an absence of words, absence of emotion and absence of feelings that fills this void in my heart. I do not contain the capacity to put this onset of emotions into words. Extreme sadness is the only emotion I can define. I wish that Matthew J. Hoffman is sentenced to serve the hardest, most uncomfortable time possible for the rest of his breathing days."

Tracy Herrmann, Jason's wife, also addressed the

judge. She noted that she was so emotional that she felt overwhelmed. Tracy related that Tina was a hardworking mother, dedicated to creating a life of happiness for her children. "Kody and Sarah were beautiful children, great students, dedicated to baseball and softball. They were two innocent children just going through life like any child should."

Tracy stated that because Jason was so overwhelmed by what happened, it was she who had to explain the tragedy to their young children, eight and five years of age. She asked, "How do you explain something so horrific to children who have been blessed to know nothing but love?" She still had not fully explained to them what happened to their cousin Sarah, except to say a bad person had taken her and that he was now in jail because of what he had done. Tracy said that she knew that Kody had been protective of his sister, and that both children had fought all they could. "However, this monster, Matthew Hoffman, was pure evil and not able to be stopped by two little children."

Tracy related that since the first day she'd learned about the incident on King Beach Drive, she'd suffered from lack of sleep, weight loss, headaches and nausea. When she did fall asleep, she was haunted by nightmares. The most consistent thing she felt was fear. Fear of being alone in the house, fear of traveling alone to town, fear for the safety of her children.

Tracy declared that Matthew Hoffman had ruined many, many lives. Not just their own friends and family, but the entire community as well. She felt sadness for all the investigators who worked countless hours on the case. She knew they would take the scars of this experience with them for the rest of their lives. Most of all, she said, she felt such a deep sadness for Sarah that at times she could not utter a word about it.

Tracy ended by saying, "I believe wholeheartedly in the United States' justice system and have faith that you will impose the maximum sentence on Matthew Hoffman."

Tina's brother Bill Herrmann gave a statement similar to those of Jason and Tracy, adding that for years to come, they would have to celebrate birthdays, family events and holidays without Tina and Kody. Bill was extremely angry at Matthew Hoffman and didn't mince his words. "You are a coward, a real piece of shit! I can only hope and pray that God takes you out soon. I hope you rot in hell, you be treated and tortured as you have done to our family member. If only the law would allow us, my brothers, Larry and I would enjoy the opportunity to dismember you alive!"

Lisa Robey, Bill's girlfriend, was just as adamant. "There is no amount of punishment that is even comparable to the heinous acts and level of brutality that Hoffmann put into the kidnapping, torturing and slaughtering of our family. If justice cannot be served here in this lifetime, he will experience it in full force when he reaches the fiery pits of hell."

Tina's mother, Barbara Herrmann, expressed, "Matthew Hoffman is not a normal human being. He's a ruthless, selfish animal who took the lives of three loving and caring individuals. He murdered them, cut them up into pieces, stuffed them all in garbage bags, and then if that was not enough, he proceeded to lower them into the hollow of a tree where they would be almost impossible to find. No mother should have to bury her baby girl and grandson at the same time."

And Larry's mother, Sarah's grandmother, Esther Maynard, related, "I cry all the time. How could I not? Sweet Kody and his mom, Tina, were taken from us in the worst possible way. I find myself shaking inside. The only way to describe this pain is to say that it's as if I were shot in the heart by a shotgun." Esther, like others, hoped that Matthew Hoffman would suffer all the torments of hell. "I beg that your days be long and full of agony as you deserve."

Belinda Thompson, Stephanie Sprang's stepmother, hoped that Hoffman would suffer hell on earth, as well as in the hereafter. She prayed that he would constantly be looking over his shoulder in prison, afraid of who might rape him or kill him. That he never know one more moment of peace.

"My wish is that you remember *I* will never forgive you. I will never forget that I look forward to the day you live eternally with the demons of hell. May you be torched and burned over and over, forever. I will hate you to the day I die for what you have done to my family and my community."

Stephanie's daughter Trisha said, "The pain I have endured is unbearable. Not only have I lost a mother who

I'll never get back, but I feel like I've lost my younger brother [Kody] for whom I've played the role of a second mom."

Trisha related that two weeks prior to the events of November 10, she and Stephanie had been squabbling, as mothers and teenage daughters often do. Trisha found it incredible now that she couldn't know then how little time she had left with her mother. "I never thought I'd lose her and become completely helpless. Everyone tries to help me, but no one can help like her. She knew what to say and how to say it."

Tracy Maynard, Larry's wife, asked Matthew Hoffman, "How could you do this to our family? How can you call yourself a human being for that matter? What kind of man preys on two innocent women and children?"

Tracy spoke of how she had to try and explain all of this to her four-year-old son, AJ, who woke up crying every day because he missed his big brother, Kody. Tracy said she had to explain that Kody and his mom Tina were now in heaven. "You have ripped my family apart mentally and physically. It's hard to go on with life since things will never be normal again and this tragedy has changed our lives forever."

Tracy was angry that because of the plea deal, Matthew continued to live on earth. That was something he'd denied to Tina, Kody and Stephanie. She added, "I hope you suffer every day like my family will, except the difference is I am human and you are not."

Larry Maynard read a portion of Matthew 18 from

the New Testament. "At that time the disciples came to Jesus and asked, 'Who then, is the greatest in the kingdom of heaven?'"

Larry related the story of Jesus calling the little child to him, and his words: "If anyone causes one of these little ones—those who believe in me—to stumble, it would be better for them to have a large millstone hung around their neck and to be drowned in the depths of the sea. Woe to the world because of the things that cause people to stumble!"

Larry said later, "I purposely picked a verse from Matthew to see how Matthew Hoffman would react to that. He didn't react at all. He just stared down at the desk in front of him."

Larry was just as angry at Matthew Hoffman as the others had been; he said in his statement, "I don't even know where to begin. My kids are my world, like most parents. On November 10, my life as I knew it changed forever. The children that Tina Herrmann and I brought into this world, Kody and Sarah Maynard, were two beautiful kids. Sarah was only four pounds, nine ounces, and six weeks premature. Kody was five pounds, seven ounces and was a preemie also.

"I could hold each one of them in the palm of my hand. When God gave me these two beautiful kids, I knew I was responsible for more than just myself. These two precious babies depended on me and looked up to me as their father. A child's bond is like no other love or bond I believe you can have with anything else on earth.

"Matthew Hoffman, when you took my son from me

by brutally stabbing him to death and then cutting up his body like a piece of meat, a majority of me died with him.

"I am very thankful my daughter lived despite the wrath of your evil. But she will never be the bubbly little innocent girl she once was. My son, Kody, was a straight-A student who had dreams of going into the Coast Guard and being a helicopter pilot. He would have saved a lot of lives. He was that type of kid. So you didn't just take him from our family, you deprived America of a great human being.

"I used to think that the parent was the teacher of children, but they taught me more about love than I ever knew existed. Matthew, my son was on this earth for eleven years, and I guarantee you, he made more of a positive impact and showed more love than you have shown in your entire life. Matthew Hoffman, you are a coward, a spawn of the devil. Any man who can harm two innocent women and two innocent kids, is a pathetic person.

"Whatever they do to you today won't even be half as much as God will do to you on Judgment Day. I hope you are cast into the fiery pits of hell, you sorry excuse for a human being. I hope you wake up every day thinking of Tina, Kody, Sarah and Stephanie. And I hope you get jailhouse justice. Maybe God can forgive some day, but I sure the hell never will!

"There isn't a night that goes by that I get much sleep. My every waking moment is spent grieving the loss of my eleven-year-old son and pain for my thirteen-year-old daughter. She has lost her mother and brother, and I wish as her father, that I could take that loss away from her.

"Every morning when I wake up, I think it is just a bad dream that someone killed my son and kidnapped my daughter. And then a couple of minutes go by, and it really sets in that this isn't a bad dream. This is reality. No more throwing a football with Kody. No more playing video games. No more baseball games. No more fishing trips, first car for graduation, college. What would his kids look like? We will never know.

"No more birthdays. A couple of weeks before this, I told him I would take him to a Cleveland Browns game. That's not going happen now. How do I explain to his four-year-old half-brother, whom he looked up to, that Kody is never coming home. I have to say, 'Son, he is in heaven with God.'

"Matthew Hoffman, you should totally be ashamed of what you did. But I do not believe you have a conscience or a heart. So with that, I hope you rot in hell, you sick bastard."

All of these people expressed their grief, anger and hatred of Matthew Hoffman. But none more so than Larry Maynard and his family. That included the one survivor of the tragedy—Sarah.

THIRTY-TWO

"I'm Not Scared of You, Matthew"

Sarah wanted to read aloud to Matthew Hoffman a letter she had written. Some, however, thought it would be too stressful and painful for her to do, so instead, Prosecuting Attorney John Thatcher read it on her behalf. Sarah sat in a black dress next to her dad as the statement was read in the courtroom.

Her letter began, "This has changed my whole life, and my family's life too.

"This is so sickening, Matthew, to know how you even had the guts to do this to this family. Stephanie was a great woman too. She watched Kody and me whenever my mom needed her to. All I'm thinking about is how sick and disgusting you are.

"I will never forget about Kody and my mom, Tina. I think Matthew is really stupid for killing the dog too.

What could we have possibly done to you, Matthew, to be treated like this? There is no reason why. Matthew, when you kidnapped me, I kept asking if you killed my mom and my brother. And you said, 'Don't worry about it.'

"How could you possibly do this to a loving and caring family? Matthew, you must have been planning this for a really long time, because you have to have skills and time to do such a thing like this. I wonder if it even goes through your head, 'Why did I do this? Now I'm going to prison for life.'

"My brother was only eleven years old and his name was Kody. My mom was thirty-two years old and her name was Tina Herrmann. My mom did a lot for Kody and me. I didn't even get to say that I loved him one last time. I told my mom before I went to school that I loved her and for her to have a good day at work.

"I'm very, very thankful for the guys who worked so hard to find me. Matthew, I don't know if you thought you were going to get away with this, but luckily didn't. I think Matthew was purposefully trying to scare me and my family, but I'm not scared of you, Matthew. I'm going to stand up for myself and live my life.

"When this happened on November 10, 2010, all I was thinking about was if my family was okay and if I was going to be able to live. Especially when he was putting the ropes on me, and I said, 'Oww, that hurts!' He said, 'I don't care if your arms and legs turn purple.'

"When I went to my room, I was going to call the police, but Matthew got in there just in time. I was so scared when Kody and I walked into the house that day and there was a huge patch of blood by the front door. My reaction was 'Oh My God!'

"Justice will never be served. I will never be able to get my mom and brother back until I see them in heaven. Kody will never ever see our family again. There is so much stress in my life right now, thinking that another idiot is going to kill me or something. Matthew, I want you to know that you will never be forgiven by me.

"Some memories of Kody: he was a left-handed pitcher and he was really good. A whole bunch of people always told him how good a player he was. In life, he wanted to be a helicopter pilot in the Coast Guard.

"Some memories of Mom: she always made sure we were happy, and she went out and did stuff with Kody and me, even though she didn't have that much money. She always made sure we had heat in our house to stay warm, made sure we had food on our plates, nice clothes on, and that we had shoes on our feet. She was a really caring woman, and when someone needed help, she would take her time to go help them. I loved her as a mother even though there were times we didn't get along. She loved dolphins and sunflowers. One thing she said to me, 'Sarah, when I die, I want you to send me with the dolphins.'

"I will tell you a little about me. I played softball for three years. I was so good at it. I played in the outfield and I played on the All-star Team over the summer. I loved it. I'm almost fourteen. I enjoy my new school and the people there!!!"

Sarah's last comment was meant as an "in-your-face"

to Matthew Hoffman, a reiteration of her ealier theme that he had not destroyed her spirit and she was no longer afraid of him. And then she brought up the fact that where he was going, *he* was the one who now had to be afraid.

Judge Eyster read each and every count and had Matthew Hoffman declare how he pleaded on the count. To each count, Hoffman said "guilty" in a fairly strong voice until it came to the sexual assault count, when Hoffman's voice could barely be heard. So the judge asked him once again how he pleaded. Hoffman this time said more loudly, "Guilty."

Larry Maynard stated later, "It was apparent he didn't want anyone to hear how he pled on that count. He didn't want that on the record, where anyone in prison could see that he had sexually molested a thirteen-year-old girl. Prisoners hate pedophiles and Hoffman knew it."

After all the pleas of guilty, Judge Eyster sentenced him to a life in prison without the possibility of parole. Hoffman was escorted out of the courtroom, and Larry Maynard recalled, "I was glad to get him out of my sight!"

After the sentencing, Larry Maynard had a few things to say to the media. He related, "It was good to get it all out in court. He [Matthew Hoffman] got what he deserved. Justice was served. We can't let him know that the victims' families will be scared. Violence will not be tolerated, and the local law enforcement did a great job."

After Hoffman's sentencing, Stephanie Sprang's mother, Pat Cullins, and sister, Sherrie Baxter, both wrote letters to Prosecuting Attorney John Thatcher, praising the work of his office. And Stephen Thompson, Stephanie Sprang's father, related, "I'm satisfied with what he got. He got what he deserved, and I'm satisfied with the results." Still, he added, "We've tried to go through [a normal] Thanksgiving and Christmas, but it's been very hard."

THIRTY-THREE

"She Would Have Been the Star Witness"

Prosecutor John Thatcher held a press conference to wrap up the case and to let the media ask questions. He introduced his assistant prosecutors, Jennifer Springer and Chip McConville, as well as Sheriff David Barber and Special Agent Joe Dietz from BCI&I. Then Thatcher went over the basic synopsis of the case once more, from Hoffman entering Tina Herrmann's home to the murders and kidnapping of Sarah Maynard. Thatcher also detailed the hunt for Sarah, her rescue, and the search for the three missing victims.

When it came to how and why the plea deal had been made with Matthew Hoffman, Thatcher said, "I take full responsibility for all the charges brought in this case. However, I thought it was right and fair to consult with the family members first. I told them of the offer and of dropping the death penalty if Matthew Hoffman would identify the location of the remains of Stephanie Sprang, Tina Herrmann and Kody Maynard.

"It was my decision to make. Anyone who has a problem with the death penalty out of this case, has a problem with me. I don't want to hear any complaints about the families. They only expressed their wishes. They didn't tell me what to do.

"I decided that the justice needed in this case was, number one—within twenty-four hours all remains would be recovered. Hoffman would then plead guilty to all charges brought in the indictment.

"I told the family that after a week of searching, it was possible the bodies would never be found. There was only one person who knew where they were. I told the family members, ultimately it was my decision to make, but I think you have the right to know.

"I asked each and every one of them how they felt. It was their wish that they find their loved ones as soon as possible. Then we could find out what he did and when he did it.

"Helping these family members find their loved ones as soon as possible, is what we did. From what I've heard, we probably never would have found those bodies in a meaningful period of time and bring some kind of closure to these families.

"They [the family members] were able to watch their television sets as three hearses took the bodies of their loved ones away. They were able to have their calling hours and funeral services—not only the family members, but the whole community. Some day there might have been that opportunity years and years in the future. But the ability to do that now at least brought some closure to these people.

"After the bodies were recovered, there were other issues. The families wanted to know, why did he choose that house? There were a lot of speculations and fears. There was a speculation that Matthew Hoffman had accomplices. They wondered if family members had been stalked—particularly Sarah.

"And frankly, the investigation, as thorough as it was, couldn't answer all the questions. Matthew Hoffman had to give those answers. So as part of the agreement, he had to make a full confession, which he did. He had to fill in the investigators with some of the missing parts that only he knew."

While others in the community, like Larry Maynard, would still hang on to their convictions that Sarah, Tina or Stephanie had been stalked by Hoffman and then everything spun out of control from there, Thatcher said that he believed Hoffman did fill in those gaps, and that it was ultimately a burglary gone bad.

Thatcher continued, "There is no indication that [Hoffman] targeted those people or stalked those people. He murdered Tina and Stephanie because they surprised him. Unfortunately, Kody and Sarah came home, and as you know, he also murdered Kody.

"For whatever reason, he decided to spare Sarah. And thank God he did. Because if he hadn't spared her life, I'm not sure we would have been able to solve this case.

His intention was to remove the bodies from the home and to burn the house down and make his escape. I think he would have eventually been caught, but we wouldn't have had the evidence at the crime scene that we were able to work with if he had decided not to spare Sarah's life. Rescuing Sarah was the only ray of sunshine in this whole situation.

"Some people have questioned my decision to include a rape charge. My explanation for it is this—in addition to being a brutal murderer, Matthew Hoffman is also a sex offender. And even though he'll never get out of prison, he will be classified as a sex offender in prison. That charge will be with him for the rest of his life. If anyone, who has had contact with the victim in this case, has any problem with that, shame on them. The victim in this case had nothing to do with putting herself in that situation. Obviously she was kidnapped and forced into that situation.

"A factor in this decision—I know that a change of venue was likely. That would have delayed a trial even longer. And at trial, the families would have to relive the situation all over again. It would have required the one living witness, Sarah, to testify in court. Now she is spared having to do that.

"I can't express how grateful I am to the state-wide law enforcement community. This is the type of situation that will overwhelm any size county. There were officers who came down here with sick children at home, and two hours' sleep, to investigate crime scenes.

"I'd like to thank everyone in our community and

outside our community who came here, who hoped we would find these three missing people alive. At the time, we were all praying we would find these people alive. It didn't turn out that way, but that doesn't diminish anything that they did."

Thatcher then threw the floor open to questions.

One reporter asked, "Was there one specific piece of evidence that led you to Hoffman?"

The response was, "Let me tell you a story that was a pretty amazing piece of detective work. There were a couple of items at the crime scene that didn't look like they belonged there. There was a shopping bag with a couple of items in it, and we used the product code identity and tracked it to a specific store." This was, of course, the Walmart store in Mount Vernon. "We saw an individual leave in a car, and were able to pull up a driver's license photo matching that individual. It turned out to be Matthew Hoffman."

A reporter wanted to know how Hoffman could have pulled off such a complex series of actions singlehandedly, since so many cars were involved. Thatcher said that after the confession, Hoffman had had to answer the investigators' questions. And the timeline he drew up about his activities matched what was believed to have been possible. There were no indications that anyone else was involved.

"How specific was [Hoffman] about where the bodies were?" another reporter asked.

"We didn't want him out of jail. So the directions were specific enough that it didn't take a lot of searching."

When asked if he knew why Hoffman had spared Sarah, Thatcher responded, "I don't think he gave any reason other than he said he just couldn't kill her. I know that statement falls pretty flat under the circumstances. But whatever it was that prevented him from taking her life, thank God that it did."

Thatcher also emphasized that if Matt Hoffman ever tried to appeal his sentencing, "then it would set the clock back to November 17, 2010, and I could ask for the death penalty once again. It would essentially be a breach of contract if he appeals the conviction and sentencing."

A final question was, "How much did Sarah help you in this case?"

Thatcher answered, "A lot. It was the effort and strength on her part to be able to relive what had been happening to her. She knew that some of the things he told her weren't true. If this case had gone to trial, she would have been the star witness. And I think she would have done a good job."

THIRTY-FOUR

The *Today Show*

The Knox County Board of Commissioners drew up a resolution to "Commend the Knox County Sheriff, Knox County Prosecutor and Knox County Public Defender regarding the horrific tragedy which recently befell Knox County."

The resolution went on to state that the commissioners commended the investigation for rescuing Sarah Maynard and for the swift capture of Matthew Hoffman. The commissioners also commended "Sheriff Barber, Prosecutor John Thatcher and Public Defender Bruce Malek for enduring difficult press conferences before an audience of mass media. The dignity and respect that they displayed towards the victims and their families was both professional and compassionate."

The resolution thanked Emergency Management Director Brian Hess for organizing and coordinating all the search efforts, and victims' advocate Diana Oswalt for her efforts in counseling the family survivors. Last, the resolution thanked every citizen volunteer who helped in the search effort.

Even an attorney from Utica, Ohio, sent a letter to Prosecutor John Thatcher and Public Defender Bruce Malek, praising them for their common sense in the matter. The letter stated, "I've always said that there is more common sense in small towns than elsewhere and your handling of this case is a good example of the application of some good old small town common sense. I surely understand that both of you were and may continue to be subjected to pressures and criticism from the public and other sources but at very least you can find comfort in knowing that you did the right thing in some very, very difficult circumstances."

Some people call the time after these types of events a period of healing—but for Larry and Sarah, it was more a time of trying to come to grips with what had happened. With scars that ran deep and wide, they knew it was not going to be an easy task. Larry had nightmares almost every night, and they were usually the same. His children were missing and he didn't know if they were cold or hungry. They were missing somewhere "out there," but he didn't know where the "there" was. He'd wake from his nightmares in a sweat, only to discover that reality was even worse than the nightmare.

As for Sarah, up until the sentencing, she would talk to her dad about what happened. Larry said, "She would always start at the beginning and go all the way through the story. It wouldn't vary. She would never just talk about one part of it. It was always the full event from beginning to end. I would just let her go on in this manner for as long as she needed to. I knew that she had to handle things this way.

"Then after the sentencing of Matthew Hoffman, it was like turning off a faucet. She stopped talking about it altogether. It was as if she was determined to put it in the past. She didn't want to waste any more energy on him. She focused on school and friends. She focused on her new family life in a new home."

Larry continued to avoid calls from news reporters and television talk shows. Bit by bit the media frenzy that had surrounded his house dissipated. This, at least, was a relief for him and his family.

Many television news programs and talk shows, however, were eager to interview Sarah and Larry Maynard on their shows. In the end, Sarah and Larry decided to be interviewed live on one show—the *Today Show* in New York. They liked the show and trusted anchor Meredith Vieira to conduct a fair and respectful interview. Larry said, "She came across as a nice person. Someone who would treat us with respect. She had a good reputation in the business and we liked the format."

In February 2011, Larry and Sarah took off for New York City. Neither one had ever been there before, and they spent some time before the interview seeing the

sights and downtown Manhattan, including the Empire
State Building. Just being in the heart of the city was
exciting for Sarah.

Later, sitting side by side on the television set of the
Today Show, Larry wore a blue dress shirt and Sarah
looked sophisticated in a black dress and white sweater.
Her hair was elegantly styled, and she looked very different from the girl who had been rescued on a bed of leaves
in Matthew Hoffman's basement.

Before the interview began, the show ran a segment
about the events of November 2010, including photos
and video clips of the story as it had developed. Then
Meredith Vieira began the interview by stating, "Sarah,
I think that you are an incredibly brave young lady given
everything that you have gone through. And I want the
audience at home to know that this is something you
wanted to do, you wanted to come forward and speak
out." Vieira said that she knew Sarah was seeing a grief
counselor in Ohio, and then asked why Sarah wanted to
be on the show that morning.

Sarah said, "To let people know how I could survive
what he did to me. So I just listened to everything he
told me to do . . ." and then her words trailed off.

Vieira picked up with, "And you got through it."
Then she asked how Sarah had stayed strong through her
days of captivity.

Sarah replied, "Just hoping someone would find me
so I wouldn't have to live with him—or stay with him
there."

Vieira then said that she knew Matthew Hoffman had

bound her hands and feet. And he also stated in his confession that he made hamburgers for her to eat. Vieira
asked, "Was he trying to befriend you, or was he constantly threatening you?"

Sarah answered, "No, I think that in that letter [Hoff-
man's confession] he was just trying to make people
think that he felt good about himself. To think that he
fed me and stuff, and he didn't. He didn't let me shower
or do any of that stuff."

Vieira asked if Hoffman had kept her down in the
basement the whole time, and Sarah said that was basically the case except for short periods in the closet and
bathroom when she'd first been taken to the house. Then
Vieira asked Larry if it had been a nightmare for him
during those four days, not knowing where his son or
daughter were, or any of the other missing people. Larry
replied, "Oh, yeah! It's still a nightmare every day knowing that part of your family's not with you."

Vieira mentioned how Matthew Hoffman's confession
stated that it was just a burglary gone bad, to which
Larry reiterated his belief that it was not. "A thief steals,
a murderer kills," he said, adding that if Hoffman had
been there merely "to burglarize the house, why did he
stake it out the way he did? Why did he purchase a knife
online a week prior to making an entrance into the
house?" Larry was sure that Hoffman's motive for entering Tina's home was not to burglarize it, but rather to
kill because he was angry at the way things had turned
out in his life. Especially about losing his job and losing
his girlfriend. And Larry also believed that Hoffman had

seen Sarah in the past, and intended all along to kidnap her. And to that end, he was able and willing to kill anyone who got in his way.

Vieira then mentioned to Sarah that she'd seen photos of Hoffman's house filled with leaves, and the strange drawings in the bathroom. She asked, "Did he say anything about why the house was filled with leaves?"

Sarah answered, "He told me that someone helped him bag the leaves. He said he wanted to make my bed comfy. So he just put leaves there so I could sleep on them."

Vieira said to Larry, "You know that the sheriff has said that Sarah is the epitome of bravery."

Larry replied, "Definitely. You know, she's even an inspiration to me. As her father, I'm supposed to be the teacher of the children, but I think she's taught me far more than I could possibly ever teach her about life."

Turning to Sarah, Vieira asked why Sarah wanted to be in court on the day that Matthew was sentenced. Sarah answered, "I wanted to tell him that I wasn't scared of him. I just wanted to get on with my life."

Vieira then asked, "What keeps you strong, Sarah, and so positive?"

Sarah replied, "Just making my life go on and not thinking of what happened in the past."

Vieira said to Sarah, "We've learned about your mom and brother, that your mom was a real hardworking lady and put you and Kody above everybody else. What do you want people to know about your mom and your brother?"

For the first time in the interview, Sarah smiled. She had been very serious up to that point. Sarah said, "My mom, she took really good care of us and made sure we had food and heat and clothes. And Kody, he was just a really good brother, even if we fought a lot."

Vieira replied to that, "Well, that's what brothers and sisters do. I know they'd be proud of you. You really are an incredible young lady."

THIRTY-FIVE

A New Beginning

As time passed, Sarah got a little better every day, though it was not all a straight line to recovery. As Larry said later, "She had good days and bad days. She would have nightmares that someone was trying to break into the house and take her away once again. I had to reassure her that was not going to happen, and I was here to protect her."

Sarah gave up softball, even though she was so good at it. It was just too painful to watch and be a part of. It reminded her not only of the life she had known and lost, but of Kody as well.

Sarah went to a new school now, with no one she had known from before, which was a double-edged sword. In some ways it was good, since there was no ever-present reminder of what had happened. No link to the everyday school life she had known right up until the afternoon of

November 10, 2010, when everything suddenly stopped. On the other hand, Sarah was still a young teenage girl in a new school, a traumatic experience for any kid. Moving somewhere new, without the friends that she had grown up with, was difficult. And despite Sarah's positive attitude and her desire to succeed in her new surroundings, to not just hide in the shadows and become the "girl those bad things happened to," for some students she would still always be "that girl." The girl who had been kidnapped. The girl whose brother and mother and neighbor had been murdered, dismembered and stuffed into a hollow tree. The girl who had been all over the news.

When Sarah began going to school in Hamilton Township, she decided to take up volleyball instead. And being athletic, she was very good at it. She liked being part of the team and commented on how each player had to assist the others. Just being on the team was a bonding experience and helped Sarah adjust to her new environment.

Sarah went to counseling sessions on a weekly basis, and they did help. So did keeping in touch with Diana Oswalt, the victims' advocate at the Knox County Prosecutor's Office. And Sarah also had something else going for her. She had some inner strength to carry on, way beyond her years. She was determined not to be destroyed by what happened to her and her family. Larry had always spoken of Sarah as being a "bubbly girl." What surprised everyone was that she was such a strong girl as well.

The "bubbly" aspect about her did help Sarah make new friends at her new school. Instead of being withdrawn, she was still outgoing and popular. Larry said, "There were times we still had to talk over the past. I would say she was seventy percent bubbly most of the time now, as opposed to ninety percent before this all happened. She was just basically an optimistic girl. She always believed in her possibilities for the future and didn't sit around moping about things. She was determined to live more for the future than the past."

Sarah said that her dream was to become a pediatrician. She loved kids and enjoyed her new younger brothers: AJ was five, and Payton only sixteen months old. It was a new start, even with them. Sarah had been the older sister to Kody; now she was the older sister to AJ and Payton. She fell into the role more naturally than might have been expected under such trying circumstances. Sarah was always goal-oriented, and being the big sister once again was important to her.

But there were some unforeseen circumstances for Larry. He said, "People who had been my friends started to drift away. They didn't know what to say to me, so they stopped coming by or calling. It was almost like we had some kind of disease that they didn't want to catch. I would wonder if they felt, 'If we get too close to him, maybe the same thing could happen to us.' I knew that was crazy, but it felt like it anyway. Matthew Hoffman had taken away my family, and now he was taking away my friends. I hated him with every ounce of my body. He was pure evil."

And both Larry and Sarah were very wary of strangers now. Their presumption of safety had been destroyed. If a man could break into Tina's house in a "safe neighborhood," then what location was safe? They viewed the world through different eyes now, experienced it in a different way.

Larry said, "Sarah would see some guy, and say, 'Dad, he looks creepy.' She was just very, very aware of her surroundings. I would not let her walk to school alone. Either I or my wife would take her there every day. We lived in a different world now."

Another new start for both Sarah and Larry was the creation of the Tina Rose B. Herrmann and Kody Alexander Maynard Healing Hearts Memorial Fund (HHMF). On the *Today Show*, Larry said of the foundation, "It's strictly a nonprofit organization developed to help victims of violent crime such as Sarah. We think it's going to be a really good organization to try and help other families that may possibly go through the same ordeal Sarah and the rest of our family has gone through." Larry said, "We wanted something good to come out of this tragedy. And it was also a way of remembering Tina and Kody and what good people they were. Kody had told me he wanted to be a Coast Guard helicopter pilot someday. He wanted to help people and rescue people. I've wondered, how many people he could have rescued in the future. Matthew Hoffman put an end to that. It's as if Hoffman killed those people who might have been saved by Kody, as well."

In May 2011, Tina's friend, Teresa Partlow, organized a raffle for the HHMF foundation. Teresa said, "Tina was a really, really good friend. She was always there to listen and always willing to help. I'm doing what I can to honor my friend."

Larry and Sarah discussed what kind of event could raise money for the Memorial Fund. As it turned out, Barbara Herrmann, Tina's mother, had a brother who was a hot air balloon enthusiast. They suggested having a hot air balloon festival in Ohio to raise money, and both Larry and Sarah thought it would be a good idea.

The Fairfield County Foundation also thought this was a good idea, and teamed up with Healing Hearts for a balloon festival in the summer of 2011. The festival would feature balloon launches and tethered balloon rides. And there would be a Sunset Glow Flight where the balloons would be illuminated in the darkness. The purpose was not only to remember the victims but also to raise money for HHMF.

Barbara Herrmann said, "We want to say to any victim of violence, it's enough going through it and surviving, but there are avenues you can turn to. It will be an honor to remember Tina and Kody. Their deaths were a tragedy, but from this tragedy, we hope we can help others." She added, "They touched so many lives when they were alive. Now they'll be able to touch people after they're gone. I also want to help people because it helps me."

On August 5, 2011, in Carroll, Ohio, the first annual hot air balloon festival took place, with eleven balloons rising into the skies. Funds were raised through sales of balloon rides, games and food. Even Sarah and Larry took a balloon ride, and Sarah was very excited by the event. A huge smile spread across her face as the balloon ascended into the air, and central Ohio spread out below her. It was as if she was leaving the troubles that haunted her back on the ground. For a little while she could soar above all of that.

Larry said later, "It was good for her. It showed me the happy girl that was so much a part of the way she always was. Sarah's doing her best, and getting better every day. She's determined not to let things get her down."

Tina's mother, Barbara Herrmann, said of her granddaughter, "She's a real live wire. Just like her mother. But all of this is still fresh in her mind. It's only been eight months since it happened." Barbara related, "This whole event was to bring something good out of something so evil. Tina's and Kody's legacy will live on through this."

After the summer ended and a new school year began for Sarah, it was amazing how well she adjusted to her new environment. She joined school activities and made lots of friends. Viewed from a distance, Sarah would look like any fourteen-year-old girl.

The psychological scars were still there, of course, but they were not overpowering. The resilience she showed was remarkable. And Sarah was lucky, in the sense that even though she had lost her mom and brother, she still had a good family who loved her and wanted the best for her. It was as normal a situation as could be possible, under the circumstances. Life went on in a rhythm that was both soothing and nurturing, a life that mirrored those of many others in their Ohio neighborhood. Sarah escaped the stigma of being "that tragic girl." She was just Sarah, and intent on being just Sarah.

She could still laugh and she could still dream. Larry talked about maybe moving to Florida someday with the family. That would put even more distance between what had happened and what the future might hold. Sarah often talked about becoming a pediatrician. Just like her mom, Tina, she loved children and wanted the best for them. Larry said, "The sky is the limit for Sarah. She's very bright and not afraid to go after what she wants in life. I'm so proud of her."

THIRTY-SIX

Bright Lights in a Sea of Darkness

On November 9, 2011, the day before the first anniversary of the tragic events that had occurred one year earlier, Larry Maynard went around Mount Vernon and Apple Valley with a journalist. They drove from Larry's home up Interstate 270 and State Highway 3 to Mount Vernon, and Larry recalled all the events of his and Tina's life. He spoke of the good times, and the rough times when he and Tina had broken up, and also the fact that they never lost respect for each other. "She was always a good person," he said. "And she loved her kids. For her, they were her whole world."

As they drove up to Columbus Road, they turned right, and then suddenly there it was—the house where Matthew Hoffman had kept his daughter, Sarah, for four days. Larry had never been there, and he struggled with his emotions as he got out of the vehicle and stood on the sidewalk in front of the house.

On the outside, it looked so ordinary. It was up for sale now, but no one was buying. Larry stared at it for a while and then said, "Sometimes I can't believe it all happened. It just seems like a bad dream and someday I'll wake up and find out that it was just a nightmare. But then I realize, it's not just a bad dream, and it did happen."

Larry walked around the house and gazed down at the basement area where Sarah had been tied up and kept on a bed of leaves. He mused, "A lot of people thought that the leaves were just a sign that he was crazy. But I believe he had another intention in mind. I think that when he was done with Sarah, he planned to kill her and then burn the house down. What could burn more quickly than dried leaves? All the evidence would be gone. He planned to burn it all down and then disappear. And he was an arsonist. He liked fires. He'd already proved in Colorado that he cared nothing about human life when he burned down that condo with people inside."

Farther around the house, a large tree loomed over Matthew Hoffman's yard. This was the tree where Hoffman had perched for hours, staring down at the neighborhood. The tree was bereft of leaves now, as it had been at this time the previous year, and the cold gray skies of November made its branches look skeletal and foreboding. Larry just gazed at it and shook his head. The thought of Matthew Hoffman up in that tree was beyond words for him.

As they came fully around the house, something suddenly caught Larry's eye, and he gasped. He pointed it out to the journalist, and they both walked up onto the front porch of the house. Someone had tied a dead squirrel to the front door handle.

Later, Larry said, "I don't know who [did that] or why they did that. Obviously, Hoffman was in prison, so he couldn't have done it. I reported it to Sheriff Barber, and he said that nothing like that was left there after the crime scene technicians had gone over the house. I have two theories about it. One is that someone left it as a sign to Hoffman, 'This squirrel shows how crazy you are.' The other theory is that someone put it there to say to everyone, 'This house is an evil place. Stay away.'"

After leaving Matthew Hoffman's house on Columbus Road, Larry and the journalist had lunch at a Mount Vernon restaurant. As they sat at their table, they could hear the quiet whispers of the other diners, sense the furtive gazes in their direction. Larry was used to this and told the reporter, "People want to say something to me, but they don't know what to say. They wonder if they should come up and give their condolences. They wonder if they should just keep quiet. It happens every day. I'm always going to be the dad of that girl who was tied up on a bed of leaves. I'm always going to be the dad of the boy who was murdered in his own home."

The restaurant was near the Knox County Sheriff's Office, and by sheer coincidence, Sheriff David Barber walked in to have lunch that same day. Larry and the sheriff shook hands and spoke for a while. "I have no doubt that Sheriff Barber and his office saved Sarah," Larry commented later. "They did everything they could to find her, Tina, Kody and Stephanie. They went full blast each and every day. They just didn't know at the time it was already too late for Kody, Tina and Stephanie. But I'll always be thankful for what all of those guys at the sheriff's office did. They were barely going home to sleep. They worked around the clock. It's what you'd hope a sheriff's office would do in a situation like this. Even they couldn't know how hard it would be. Nothing like this had ever happened around here before."

After lunch, Larry and the reporter went out to Tina's home on King Beach Drive. It sat empty now, also up for sale, but like Matthew Hoffman's home, with no buyers. On the outside it looked serene, as if nothing bad had ever happened there. Down the hill, Apple Valley Lake looked pleasant and inviting.

Larry pointed out the porch area that someone had inexplicably tried to set on fire. He also pointed to Sarah's former bedroom, where she had tried to call 911 before Matthew Hoffman restrained her—the same room where he had knifed Stephanie Sprang to death.

In the front yard, numerous items were still stacked around a tree as a memorial to the previous year's tragedy. There were stuffed animals, balloons, toys and baseballs. Especially baseballs, in memory of what a good pitcher Kody had been.

Larry said, "The stuff gets picked up every so often and taken away, but then new items appear. This has gone on all year long since November 2010. I guess there's more now, since it's almost the one-year anniversary."

Around that anniversary time, Larry and his family participated in various events to help raise funds for the Healing Hearts Foundation. One event was at the Blue Jackets Nationwide Arena in Columbus, Ohio. There, Sarah met and was photographed with the team mascot, Stinger. Later, a dinner was provided courtesy of the Front Street Restaurant.

Another event was a softball tournament at the Pipesville Road baseball fields where Kody had once played, and where Matthew Hoffman left Sarah in the Jeep with the body bags when he went on his various missions. There was a pitching contest and a home-run derby.

Sarah had also recently spoken to a reporter from WBNS who wanted to know how she was adjusting at her new school and what kinds of things she liked to do these days. Sarah said, "I love volleyball. I serve and play first row and switch out with another girl. It's a fun sport to communicate with others. And you need skills that you don't necessarily have in other sports.

"I like music and love to swim in the summertime. Like going to the beach at Myrtle Beach in South Carolina. And shopping. I'd like to get a cell phone for Christmas. She also expressed a wish to go to San Diego, California, someday. She was entranced by the thought of being on its beaches and going to its world-famous zoo.

Asked about how she felt now that nearly a year had

passed, Sarah said, "I'm usually pretty happy all the time. But going to the new school was kind of hard. I didn't know anyone, but I adapted fast. Lots of kids came up to me, asking me if I was the new kid. And they became my friends."

The reporter noted how observant Sarah was about people around her. She noticed everything, from what they had in their hands, to their clothing and shoes. Sarah agreed that she was now very aware of her surroundings at all times. She wasn't afraid to be out in crowds, but she had a very heightened sense of awareness at all times in public.

Then the reporter said, "From the moment you got home [on November 10, 2010] you remembered everything vividly, didn't you?"

At this question, Sarah began to tear up, and the smile disappeared. It was as if she'd been thrust right back to that day and time. She began to cry and her voice quavered. A box of tissues was called for, and she used several of them. It was obvious that, beneath the surface, the memories were still deep and dark. After all, she was still only a fourteen-year-old girl, one who'd experienced a nightmare beyond belief.

Perhaps the most evocative and heartfelt event commemorating the anniversary of that horrible day was a candlelight vigil held on Apple Valley Lake at sunset on November 10, 2011. As darkness came on, scores of people arrived from all over the area to meet with Sarah and remember Stephanie Sprang, Tina Herrmann and Kody Maynard.

It was a brisk autumn night, and everyone was bundled up against the chill as the breeze blew off the lake. Suddenly, Sarah spotted Sheriff David Barber in the crowd. With a burst of exuberance she ran up and gave him a big hug, and shouted with delight, "Sheriff!" She held him tightly for a moment, knowing how much he and his office had done to rescue her.

Then Sarah, the sheriff, Larry and his family, and everyone else present lit small candles, placed them in small containers and set them adrift on the lake—dozens of small candles bobbing up and down on the ripples. If Kody, Tina and Stephanie were looking down from above, they would have seen a dazzling sight—so many tiny flickering lights of hope in a sea of darkness.

Robert Scott is the author of eighteen true-crime books, which have sold nearly a half-million copies worldwide. He has been featured on such television true-crime channels as truTV, E!, and Investigation Discovery. He is a member of several national journalistic associations.

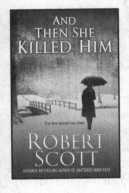